Managing suppliers and partners for the academic library

David Ball

with contributions from
Jane Ryland and Jill Beard

facet publishing

© David Ball 2005

Published by
Facet Publishing
7 Ridgmount Street
London WC1E 7AE

Facet Publishing is wholly owned by CILIP: the Chartered Institute of Library
and Information Professionals.

First published 2005

British Library Cataloguing in Publication Data
A catalogue record for this book is available from the British Library.

ISBN 1-85604-547-1

Typeset from author's disk in 11/14 Elegant Garamond and Humanist by Facet
Publishing.
Printed and made in Great Britain by MPG Books Ltd, Bodmin, Cornwall.

To my father, Alan Ball,
who loved books and died as this one
was being completed.

Contents

Contributors

David Ball
David Ball is University Librarian and Acting Head of Academic Services at Bournemouth University. He is a Board Member of the South West Museums, Libraries and Archives Council, and a leading practitioner in the field of library purchasing. He has led a number of research and digitization projects, such as the NOF-funded Dorset Coast Digital Archive. Previous experience includes work in the private sector, as information manager for a major newspaper publisher.

Jill Beard
Jill Beard is Deputy University Librarian at Bournemouth University, where her responsibilities include the development of support for the academic community, whether based on or off campus. In partnership with two local hospital trusts and the Royal College of Nursing, she collaborated in the founding of the British Nursing Index and is its Executive Director. Her research interests focus mainly on health information; she recently led a research project called Healthinfo4u to enable access to the full text of health journals by the general public.

Jane Ryland
Jane Ryland is the Academic Services Regional Support Co-ordinator at Bournemouth University. She joined the University in 1998 as Subject Librarian for Services Management. Her current role is dedicated to co-ordinating library, learning and ICT support for students studying at the University's partner institutions. Previous experience includes health and public libraries in the UK, and also in Australia and the USA.

Introduction

Universities are confronted by fundamental changes on two fronts. Firstly, the context of higher education is changing, with greater emphasis on widening participation; increasingly the learner is placed at the centre and the accent is on flexibility of learning, particularly lifelong learning. Secondly, the electronic revolution is beginning to bite in earnest. Educational technology is undergoing a step-change, as e-learning starts to become widespread: most institutions are implementing virtual learning environments. University libraries have to embrace these changes and remodel their services accordingly.

Technology is, of course, also revolutionizing both the availability of information, the university library's stock in trade, and the means of delivering it. The book has been a stable information technology for the past 500 years, the journal for 350. The means of acquiring, storing and exploiting books and journals have been correspondingly stable. The advent of electronic information has changed both the form and the means of delivery; it has also introduced completely new relationships and challenges for those concerned with the acquisition and exploitation of information.

The changes in the educational context will increasingly require universities to enter strategic and long-term relationships with external institutions, such as, in the United Kingdom (UK), further education colleges and the National Health Service, as well as with other universities. The changes in the information context necessitate new relationships between libraries and the creators, suppliers and users of information. These new relationships with suppliers continue and strengthen the trend over the last 30 years, evident in libraries as in all services and industries, away from monolithic organizations that carry out all functions in-house, towards concentrating on the core business and contracting out the rest.

Corporate and commercial relationships with external organizations are therefore becoming as important for university libraries as relationships with internal users and stakeholders. This book, for the first time, takes a comprehensive view of the main commercial and corporate relationships that university libraries enter, examines their changing nature, and suggests strategies and techniques for managing them.

The higher education context

It is difficult, if not impossible, to divorce higher education (HE) from its cultural and political context; much of this discussion concentrates on the British context. However, many of the issues, for instance widening participation, will be common to other countries and their effects of relevance to all those involved in university libraries.

Like the rest of British society, the HE sector has experienced radical change since the start of the 1960s. At that time there were 24 universities in the UK, with 120,000 students drawn chiefly, in England at least, from public and grammar schools. In 1963 the Robbins Report (Committee on Higher Education, 1963) triggered a huge expansion in the numbers of universities and students. The main principle espoused was that 'higher education opportunities should be available to all those who are qualified by ability and attainment to pursue them and who wish to do so'. To accommodate the expansion, completely new universities, such as Kent and Warwick, were created, and colleges of advanced technology, such as Salford and Strathclyde, became universities.

In 1969 a new element was added, with the foundation of the Open University. Aimed at mature students who had not followed the standard route from school to university, it delivered distance learning through a combination of technology (television and sound recordings), printed course materials, local tutorials and summer schools.

The start of the 1970s saw the creation of the new breed of polytechnics – vocationally oriented local authority institutions, generally formed from existing technical colleges, offering a wide range of further education (FE) and higher education, and focused on teaching rather than research. The polytechnics did not have degree-awarding powers; instead all graduates were awarded a degree by the Council for National Academic Awards. This produced the so-called binary system of HE, which continued until 1992, when the polytechnics were accorded university status and the two sectors, embodying the so-called 'old' and the 'new' universities, were combined.

The transition to mass HE envisaged by Robbins was not achieved without stresses and strains on the system. By the mid-1990s there were 1.6 million students in HE, more than a ten-fold increase since the publication of the Robbins Report. By 1993 the Government felt that the rise in numbers had been too rapid and introduced a cap on publicly funded undergraduate numbers, withdrawing the majority of capital funding and requiring reductions in unit costs per student.

In the 20 years from the mid-1970s, the number of students had more than doubled; public funding for HE had increased in real terms by only 45%; the unit of funding per student had fallen by 40%, while public spending on HE as a percentage of gross domestic product had remained static.

The Dearing Report

The Government's response to these problems was to set up the National Committee of Inquiry into Higher Education, chaired by Sir Ron (later Lord) Dearing. Its report, *Higher Education in the Learning Society* (1997), was to have far-reaching effects. Its terms of reference were 'to make recommendations on how the purposes, shape, structure, size and funding of higher education, including support for students, should develop to meet the needs of the United Kingdom over the next 20 years'.

The vision articulated in the report is of a society committed to learning throughout life, with 'the historic boundaries between vocational and academic education breaking down . . . [and] increasingly active partnerships between higher education institutions (HEIs) and the worlds of industry, commerce and public service'. Demand and the national need were predicted to drive a resumed expansion in student numbers, requiring HE, among other things, to:

- encourage and enable all students to achieve beyond their expectations
- be at the leading edge of practice in effective learning and teaching
- undertake research that matches the best in the world
- ensure support to regional and local communities at least matching that of competitor nations
- be accountable to students and society and seek continuously to improve its performance.

The aim of HE was to sustain a learning society; the four main purposes constituting this aim were to:

- inspire and enable individuals to develop their capabilities to the highest potential levels throughout life
- increase knowledge and understanding for their own sake and to foster their application to the benefit of the economy and society
- serve the needs of an adaptable, sustainable, knowledge-based economy at local, regional and national levels
- play a major role in shaping a democratic civilized society.

The Report called for the UK to match the HE participation rates of other competitor nations; the rate of 45% already achieved in Northern Ireland and Scotland should be the UK average. It was recognized that participation by the lower socio-economic groups, the disabled and ethnic minorities needed to be increased, and the Report suggested that funding should be targeted on those institutions demonstrating a commitment to widening participation. The expansion at undergraduate level should be matched by expansion of taught higher degrees to support lifelong learning.

Much of the expansion should be at sub-degree level – two-year courses offered overwhelmingly in further education colleges (FECs). Concerns were raised about the quality of provision through the so-called franchising of programmes by universities to FECs, and greater quality control of franchising arrangements called for.

While the Report called for continuing support for world-class research in HE in the UK, it also envisaged a radical change in attitudes to teaching, establishing HE teaching as a profession in its own right having equal status with research. This was the corollary of placing students at the centre of the vision for HE.

One mechanism suggested for making institutions more responsive to the needs of students was to channel a progressively increasing proportion of funding for tuition through the students themselves. The report accepted the principle of income-contingent contributions by graduates to both tuition and living costs.

The Government's response to the Dearing Report was generally very favourable. The vision of the Department for Education and Employment (1998) had HE playing a key role in lifelong learning and making a bigger future contribution by increasing and widening participation, particularly from groups under-represented in HE; offering opportunities later in life; increasing HE's contribution to the economy and responsiveness to the needs of business; collaborating more closely and effectively with other institutions and 'the world of work'; exploiting new technology and flexible delivery for accessibility and efficiency. The vision was founded on the idea of a compact between universities, individual students, the world of work and society.

The Future of Higher Education

The vision was elaborated in the Department for Education and Skills' White Paper, *The Future of Higher Education* (2003). The White Paper notes that the participation rate of 43% in England is low compared with many other developed countries and should be increased. However, that increase should arise, firstly, from a fundamental shift towards lifelong learning, to refresh knowledge and upgrade skills; secondly, from making work-focused courses more attractive to students and employers; and thirdly, from improving access for those under-represented.

The sector as whole is seen to have embraced lifelong learning, research excellence, knowledge transfer to business, social inclusion and regional economic development. It is now recognized that it is not possible for individual institutions to sustain all of these activities at high levels of excellence, and institutions are encouraged to focus their missions on particular activities, such as research or linking to the local and regional economy, allied in all to excellence in teaching and widening participation. This diversification is seen as decreasing competition between universities and fostering collaboration.

The vision is of a sector that:

- acknowledges and celebrates differences between institutions
- builds strong and purposeful collaboration, within HE and within FE
- is expanding towards 50% participation for those aged between 18 and 30 from all backgrounds, and providing courses satisfying both students and employers
- meets the needs of students for new modes of study and delivery of courses
- offers, in an echo of the Robbins Report, opportunity to all those with the potential to benefit
- has sufficient funding from a range of sources to sustain the sector and individual universities, based on an equitable partnership between the taxpayer, the student and others.

The keys to delivering the vision are greater explicit differentiation between institutions, greater freedom and greater collaboration.

The drive towards differentiation is evident in the intention to target resources, by rewarding research institutions adequately while steering 'non-research intensive institutions' towards other parts of their mission and rewarding them properly. The relationship between research and teaching is held to be indirect, with some of the best teaching occurring in circumstances that are not research intensive. The White Paper also encourages collaboration between institutions and particularly within regions.

The emphasis on the regional dimension is also evident in the vision for relations with business and the wider community. HEIs are seen as key drivers for their regions, economically and in terms of social and cultural contribution to their communities; it is recommended that they should increasingly be embedded in their regional economies and closely linked with their Regional Development Agencies. The potential contribution to the development of the public sector, particularly the National Health Service (NHS), is also recognized.

A major offering to business is the two-year foundation degree, where it is expected that employers will play a role in designing the courses. Again there is an equal emphasis on the public sector, where the NHS is characterized as 'one of the world's largest learning organizations', with every employee having five years' service being now entitled to training and development leading to a foundation degree. As participation increases towards 50% of those aged 18 to 30, it is expected that the bulk of expansion will be through foundation degrees. It is recognized that there will be a barrier of unfamiliarity and suspicion; financial incentives for both HEIs and students are planned.

FECs are seen as the main route for delivering foundation degrees. They already deliver 11% of HE, mainly in sub-degree programmes. Their particular strengths are portrayed as providing ladders of progression for those pursuing vocational routes, and serving part-time students and those who want to study locally. It is noted that the quality assurance of such extended provision through FECs needs to be robust and is best achieved though structured partnerships between FECs and HEIs.

FECs also play a major role in widening participation by supporting under-represented groups. This is not only through the foundation degree, but also by offering local opportunities to those studying part-time. Flexibility of learning opportunities, particularly for those in work, is also stressed.

Realizing the vision

The vision set out in the White Paper is echoed in the strategic and corporate plans of the funding bodies for the four home nations.

The Higher Education Funding Council for England (HEFCE), in its strategic plan for 2003-8 (2004a, 7), states that through funding support:

> We will help to develop a system where excellence in teaching and knowledge transfer is as highly regarded as excellence in research. We will support innovative ways of delivering lifelong learning . . . We will support institutions that reach out beyond their traditional student base to encourage those who can benefit from higher education to do so. We will support diversity, collaboration and complementary patterns of working in the drive to improve quality.

HEFCE identifies four core strategic aims – widening participation and fair access, enhancing excellence in learning and teaching, enhancing excellence in research and enhancing the contribution of HE to the economy and society – and a number of cross-cutting supporting aims, including building on institutions' strengths.

All HEIs are encouraged to widen participation, partly by working with new partners, such as the NHS and local authorities, and building on links with local communities. Foundation degrees, generally delivered in FECs, are identified as the main vehicle for continuing expansion and widening participation; together with part-time programmes they will receive a 10% funding premium. Part-time and mature students are to be encouraged, partly through vocational qualifications and workplace learning.

All HEIs are required to be excellent in teaching, and it is emphasized that excellence in teaching and learning should have the same status as excellence in research. Particularly with the increasing diversity of modes and methods of learning, including networked, mobile and workplace learning, robust quality assurance arrangements are essential. It is recognized, however, that progress has been made in the sector towards robust internal arrangements. Investment in human and physical infrastructure is acknowledged to be important, especially in the vocational sector and in partnerships between HEIs and FECs. Collaboration with local and regional employers is seen as central to delivering expansion and increased take-up of foundation degrees. Collaboration between institutions and with other stakeholders is also vital to tailor provision to regional needs.

All institutions are expected, in conjunction with other HEIs and local, regional and national partners, to enhance their engagement with business and communities. They should become fully embedded in their regional economies, working in partnership with FECs, Learning and Skills Councils and the Regional Development Agencies, and seek opportunity for engagement with business, the public sector and the wider community.

Excellent research is seen as a major factor in global competitiveness, and robust assessments of research quality are held to be fundamental to concentrating funding to support and promote excellence. HEFCE is also committed to supporting and fostering collaboration within and between institutions.

Not all institutions are expected to focus on research, and HEFCE is committed to 'supporting institutions to focus on achieving excellence in what they do best and to collaborate based on their strengths'. Specific mention is made of some HEIs developing specialisms as centres for knowledge transfer and intensive engagement with business and the community in regions, sub-regions or sectors. Support will be given to institutions repositioning themselves and establishing strong collaborative relationships.

Scotland

Responsibility for education is devolved from Westminster to Scotland where there are important historical differences from the English system, such as the broader base of secondary qualifications and the three-year ordinary and four-year honours degrees. There are also newer differences: in particular, tuition fees are not paid by students. However, there are many similarities and echoes in terms of strategy adopted.

Most marked perhaps is the recognition of the closeness of higher and further education. This has led to the Scottish Executive announcing the merger of the Scottish Higher and Further Education Funding Councils. The *Joint Corporate Plan* of the Scottish Funding Councils for Further and Higher Education (2003) also emphasizes workforce development and the need for responsiveness to employers' needs, the increased demand for post-experience learning, such as continued professional development, and for flexible forms of learning provision. Its three main aims are:

• the improvement of learning and skills to enable individuals to contribute to economic, civic and cultural life

- to ensure that the benefits of learning are open to all and that the barriers to participation and progression in and through further and higher education are removed
- the creation and transfer of knowledge for the benefit of the economy and wider society.

This book

It will be clear from the above discussion that HE in the UK is undergoing some far-reaching changes. The context within which university libraries operate will clearly offer many challenges, as their parent institutions adapt by forging new specialisms and collaborative relationships. The following chapters are an attempt to help university librarians to navigate through some of the complexities.

This book falls into two main parts. The first part deals with relationships arising from the commercial environment within which university libraries across the world are operating.

Chapter 2 analyses the information chain – its fluidity and economics as electronic information starts to dominate. Attention is paid both to the cultural and economic factors affecting the development of the electronic journal, and to the emerging business models of the e-book. It is only through developing a full understanding of the information chain that librarians will be able to control the relationships to which it gives rise. Chapter 3 looks in detail at these relationships, treating both the trends to supplier selection and shelf-ready supply of hard-copy materials, and some of the challenges associated with electronic resources, such as licence constraints and the implications of the so-called big deal. The picture for electronic resources is rounded out with a discussion of library management systems and virtual learning environments, and the requirement for these systems to interact with each other and the systems of information providers.

Chapter 4 offers practical techniques and strategies for managing suppliers, discussing in detail the five stages of the procurement cycle and how procurement consortia can operate to manage and develop the marketplace. The relatively recent but increasingly frequent phenomenon of outsourcing and externalization of service provision, to both commercial suppliers and other libraries, is examined in Chapter 5. Lessons are drawn from the public library sector; the chapter also offers a weighted decision matrix for determining whether services are suitable for outsourcing.

The second part of the book examines relationships arising directly from the academic environment within which university libraries exist. Widening participation and distance and part-time learning are major features of HE today; they are addressed in Chapters 6 and 7.

Chapter 6 deals with relationships between universities and further education colleges. Already providing 11% of HE, the FECs will become even more important as expansion is delivered through their work-focused foundation degrees. Not only are they a vehicle for enhancing HE's offering to employers; they are also fundamental to widening participation, delivering learning locally and with well developed support for those unused to HE.

In the UK, 5% of the employed population works in the National Health Service, characterized as one of the world's largest learning organizations. Already a major consumer of HE, the National Health Service will become even more important as its non-clinical workforce pursues foundation degrees and continuing professional development. Chapter 7 examines in some detail relationships with the NHS as probably the most complex and common manifestation of the challenge of providing work-based learning. Together, Chapters 6 and 7 cover the challenges related to delivering services to learners who are at a distance, in the workplace and part-time.

Chapter 8 closes the second part of the book by looking at library collaboration in its many forms, focusing particularly on regional collaboration, which is a major thread running through the developing strategy for HE in the UK. Much collaboration is delivered through project working, and the chapter closes by outlining some of the main techniques of project management.

2
The information chain

Introduction

Libraries are essentially purveyors of information to their clienteles. The information world in which they operate is in a state of flux: e-journals have become an established resource in the academic world; e-books will shortly become widely used in the UK; free electronic resources, such as government statistics, are becoming increasingly important. Business models for many of these resources have yet to stabilize. Is the big deal for electronic journals a transitory or permanent phenomenon? How do we buy e-books? It is therefore important for the academic librarian to grasp the fundamentals of the information value chain as they affect commercial relationships and to understand the implications for the educational context, particularly for the delivery of flexible and distance learning and the introduction of virtual learning environments.

This chapter discusses the economics underlying publication, especially:

- the information value chain and some of its concepts, paying particular attention to features differentiating electronic from printed information
- electronic journals, including open access journals and institutional repositories
- the emerging supply chain and business models for e-books.

The information value chain
Concepts

Following the useful taxonomy of Bide (1998), the information supply chain comprises essentially the following activities or functions: creation, publication, aggregation, access and use. To a greater or lesser degree, each of the activities, or links, adds value to the information, until it is used and the value realized. This account is somewhat simplified: it does not discuss exhaustively the roles of all the players in the chain, but concentrates on the key ones.

Branding and authority

Each link in the chain confers an element of branding or authority on the information. Branding has to do with consistency and quality. Examples might be Coca-Cola and Pepsi Cola: these are different brands, with different qualities, consistent in themselves and having different adherents. Authority has to do with reliability, informed opinion, having status or expertise. One thinks for instance of the BBC: a news broadcast in the World Service carries a great deal of authority.

Monopoly

Each link in the chain also has a greater or lesser degree of monopoly. This is obviously particularly important for the information marketplace. This chapter highlights where monopolies and competition lie, since sometimes they can be used to advantage, and sometimes they cause the purchaser or user problems.

The product-to-service shift

One major factor differentiating electronic from printed information is the shift from product to service. With printed information, much labour and cost are tied up in producing, distributing, storing and handling a physical product: books and serials. With electronic information, libraries and other intermediaries generally deal only in access to information held in a remote location, a service not a product. It is worth noting that this shift follows a general trend, as companies and public bodies outsource more and more activities.

Creation

Creation is a familiar concept, and needs no long discussion. Creators may be authors or compilers. They may be directly employed by publishers, as are journalists and technical writers. Alternatively, they may be independent of the publishers, working as professional authors or academics.

Particularly in popular fiction, the creator confers authority. One obvious example is Stephen King: one knows what one is getting when picking one of his novels from the shelf. On the cover, it is his name, not the title, that has prominence. The creator is also a monopolist: only Stephen King produces his novels. This monopoly, protected by copyright, is then generally transferred to a single publisher.

Publication

Publication is essentially concerned with the selection and editing of information into consumable form. In one sense, it is a form of quality control. Publishers also package information into usable and buyable units (titles, series, journals), market the product, and undertake, or subcontract, physical production and distribution.

For librarians, authority is conferred in part at least by the imprint – Oxford University Press, for instance, or Butterworths. The end-user is more likely to focus on the brand – *British Medical Journal*, *Nature* or *Who's Who*. This holds equally true for academic publications, where the editorial and refereeing process is concentrated at the level of the title, as for general publications.

The publisher's monopoly, often transferred from the creator, is also jealously preserved.

For those involved in academic libraries, the delivery of information in electronic form embodies some important differences from delivery in printed form. There is essentially no physical production and distribution of electronic information. There is a physical realization at the moment of use – as an image on a computer screen or as a printout – but this occurs only at the end of the information chain, not close to the origin, as happens with print. With the electronic form, the rest of the chain deals in access to the information, not in a physical product containing the information. Librarians, as purchasers, are therefore now buying a service as opposed to a physical product.

One should also note that, with electronic information, authority is potentially diluted. It is easy to publish and disseminate information on the web, far easier than publishing and disseminating in print, which require considerable investment of money and time. It has become correspondingly difficult to establish the authenticity and provenance of information. What is the status of the author, and of the publishing institution, if any? Has there been a process of peer review and editing? If so, how rigorous has it been? Has it been applied to the personal web pages of members of an institution?

Aggregation

One may define aggregation as 'bringing together in a coherent collection disparate information sources'. Clearly, this is core territory for the information professional. The traditional activity of acquisition that formed our large historic libraries is now increasingly underpined by the procurement process and the support and expertise of procurement professionals, who are bringing greater regulation and management into this process and increasing value for money for their institutions.

Libraries confer authority by virtue of selecting material. Users, whether students or members of the public, perceive a certain warranty of fitness for purpose if a book is on their library's shelves: the library is a brand that they trust. Libraries also have a perhaps unrecognized near monopoly on such aggregations of printed information. There are few alternatives, except a bookshop, where stock, facilities and opportunities for consultation and loan are severely limited or impossible.

It is important to note in this context the accent on the physical product. Much of a traditional library's work is concentrated on acquiring, processing, protecting and handling these physical products. Increasingly, as far as the acquisitions process goes, this is subcontracted or outsourced to intermediaries, such as booksellers or serials agents.

With electronic information, there is no physical product to acquire or handle. The role of aggregator may therefore move elsewhere in the supply chain, to the publisher or an intermediary such as the serials agent. There is also a trend to 'virtual' aggregation, with services such as CrossRef, where the articles of major serials publishers are linked, while remaining on servers run by the publishers themselves. A similar role is played by search engines such as Yahoo!, which bring together websites in subject categories.

The libraries' collective near monopoly, evident for printed information, is therefore lost: users need set foot nowhere near a library to have access to aggregators' sites; they simply need a network connection and either the appropriate permissions or deep pockets. This cold wind of loss is also felt by the commercial aggregators with whom libraries deal, booksellers and serials agents. Booksellers are losing custom both to electronic alternatives available free or for a fee from websites, and to virtual bookshops such as Amazon. Some publishers are insisting that libraries buy bundles of electronic journals direct from them, and not through serials agents.

Access

Facilitating and controlling access to aggregated printed information is again core territory for libraries, needing little explication. Selective dissemination of information raises awareness. Catalogues, bibliographies and indexes aid discovery and location. User education, particularly in academic libraries, trains users in gaining efficient access to and effectively exploiting information. Library management systems control access to collections. The libraries' monopoly on providing access and the tools that support it is again generally unrecognized.

Providing access to electronic information is, however, fundamentally different. One prerequisite is a robust IT infrastructure to deliver the information. In the UK, this infrastructure is well established in academic libraries and is widespread now following recent investment in the public library sector. Many users have their own PCs and internet connections. Soon set-top boxes will deliver internet connectivity through the television screen. Provision and installation of such set-top boxes may follow the pattern established by mobile phone companies, which gave away the hardware in order to be able to sell services. Libraries therefore are fast losing the monopoly on access: the majority of users may soon be able to connect to information resources more easily from their living rooms than from a terminal in a library.

Search engines, such as Google, Ask Jeeves and Yahoo!, offer user-friendly but increasingly sophisticated information retrieval from millions of web pages. They offer services paralleling the catalogues, bibliographies and indexes that are standard provision in academic libraries, but with some important differences. They have the advantage of providing immediate access to a wealth of current information impossible to find in a single traditional hard-copy library; but they also have the drawback of offering no warranty of the provenance and standing of the information accessed.

Competition extends beyond information retrieval. One can foresee existing providers of online services offering alternative public information services too. It is common commercial practice to extend one's brand into different product areas: Virgin's expansion from record retailer to airline is one obvious example, the provision of financial and insurance services by supermarkets another. Information provision may not be immune to this practice. In the academic context, one supplier of e-books deals only with end-users, not libraries. One 'quotation' on its website from a satisfied customer reads: 'I got an A+ using this library. It's so much easier than the regular library.'

The libraries' collective near monopoly on providing and facilitating access to information is therefore lost. Authority is also diluted. How far can one trust the information offered as an add-on by a commercial service-provider, or the provenance of websites found through a search engine? For the time being libraries will retain the authority conferred by their traditional roles as selectors and organizers of information resources. Their more recently acquired role as educators, inculcators of information literacy, will become even more important in helping readers to stay afloat on and navigate the ocean of information now available to them.

Use

The end of the chain, and its reason for existence, is the user, who, of course, particularly in the academic sector, may also be the start of the chain.

Hitherto it has been stressed that, for traditional printed resources, libraries have dealt with a physical product. What they have always provided to the user is a service – access to the information – not the physical product itself. Even in the case of photocopies, a little thought should demonstrate that this is so: the product is returned to the shelf.

Here is also one of the conundrums of the information chain. How, particularly in the print environment, does one measure actual usage of acquired stock? Librarians routinely collect statistics on loans, footfall, etc., but these statistics do not fully reflect actual usage. Of five items borrowed, only one may be used; the rest may not be needed for whatever reason. There is also the challenge of effectively measuring reference usage within the library, something that is very difficult to achieve regularly and accurately.

There is a further problem: not only do measures of usage tend to be blunt and unsophisticated, they also do not reflect the actual value of usage to the reader. Of five items borrowed or consulted, only one may be of value. If one cannot demonstrate value to the user, it is very difficult to justify purchasing decisions.

Holding information electronically offers some help here: it opens the possibility of recording and measuring usage more accurately, as expressed in access to and downloads of particular texts or services. It is also possible to envisage systems of payment for such usage, either through actual cash transactions or through users having and exchanging a number of credits. Holding information electronically therefore opens the way to more accurate measures of both usage by, and value to, the end-user.

Electronic journals

Commercial journal publishers led the way in moving to electronic format. This section discusses the underlying economics of journal publishing and examines the new possibilities offered by open access publishing and institutional repositories, which in theory have the potential to undermine commercial academic journal publishing.

Money as an indicator of value

It is worth taking a little time to chart the flow of money through the value chain, and to reflect on where it sticks.

Creation, dissemination and validation

Beginning with the independent creator (i.e. one not employed to write) it is evident that in popular fiction the rewards tend to go to the author. Stephen King and Tolkien are commodities: their creativity is the point of scarcity, and points of scarcity tend to attract money.

Scholarly and academic authors, on the other hand, are generally paid nothing, or next-to-nothing, for their output. Scholarly journals obviously cannot exist without their output, but this dependence is not recognized in economic terms. It is the publisher, not the author, who reaps the direct financial rewards of publication. This is reflected, for instance, in the profits of the big academic publishers. Thus Houghton (2000, 65) notes:

> in 1997 Reed Elsevier enjoyed a higher net profit margin than 473 of the S&P 500 listed companies, Wolters Kluwer provided higher return on equity than 482 of the S&P 500, and margins generated in the science, technical and medical publishing areas of the companies tend to be even higher than aggregate margins.

So what are they rewarded for? Publishers in effect provide two services:

1 They disseminate information.
2 They confer authority by ensuring quality.

Dissemination can be achieved by anyone with a network connection: scholars and professionals regularly use e-mail and other similar means of disseminating results; many academics now have their own web pages, where they make available their papers. Dissemination is not therefore a point of scarcity. This conclusion is supported by an examination of the rewards of intermediaries, which shows an interesting difference between booksellers and serials agents. Booksellers are a much more valued part of their supply chain. They can command very high discounts from the publisher, particularly for popular fiction, where authority or branding derives from the author. Thus, in some supermarkets we see discounts of 50% off the prices of popular books. Serials agents, on the other hand, command very low margins on hard copy – an average of 7% has been cited.

One may conclude that scholarly publishing in academic journals is essentially about validation of results through the editorial and peer-review process rather than dissemination. Guédon (2001, 3) traces this process of validation, of creating the scholarly record, of establishing paternity and property rights, back to the 17th century, where it is already evident in the first issues of the *Philosophical Transactions of the Royal Society of London*.

Reaping the rewards

Scholarly and academic authors do in fact reap indirect rewards from publication. Publication, particularly in prestigious peer-reviewed journals, leads to promotion and to research funding. There is, of course, institutional, as well as personal, interest in such publication: the funding and prestige of institutions are generated in large measure by their scholars. This institutional interest is particularly evident in the UK, where the quinquennial Research Assessment Exercise ranks university departments and, in order to foster excellence in research, disburses large sums of money to the best. One major indicator in the ranking process is publication in respected peer-reviewed journals.

There is clearly a large financial interest, on the part of both individual scholars and their employing institutions, in continuing to play the game of scholarly publication in existing established peer-reviewed journals; this may explain, in part at least, why new electronic initiatives outside traditional publishing have not taken off. Academic publishers claim the direct financial rewards by virtue of fulfilling a need of scholars and institutions for validation. Their monopoly has allowed them to inflate prices, unchecked by a market where the user is insulated from the effects of inflation.

There have been protests over a number of years about the price rises imposed by commercial publishers, not only from librarians but also more interestingly from academics on editorial boards. Editors and whole boards have resigned to set up alternative rival publications. Examples are *Vegetatio*, which in 1989 engendered *Vegetation Science*, *Evolutionary Ecology Research*, which engendered *Evolutionary Ecology* in 1998, and the *Journal of Logic Programming*, which engendered *Theory and Practice of Logic Programming* in 1999 (Key Perspectives, 2004, 6).

The above remained within the arena of commercial publishing, albeit in at least one instance moving from a purely commercial publisher to a publisher within the academic ambit. It is only the advent of the modern electronic technologies that has threatened to subvert commercial publishing. There are two main ways in which scholarly articles can be made freely available to potential readers: publication in an open access journal or deposit in an institutional or subject repository.

Open access journals and institutional repositories

The open access journal has been defined, in its simplest terms, as one 'not charging readers or their institutions for the right to access, download, copy, print, distribute or search the articles' (Thomson ISI, 2004, 1).

It is generally agreed that the first free fully peer-reviewed open access journal was *Psycoloquy*, edited by Stevan Harnad, which appeared in 1989, followed shortly afterwards by *Surfaces*, edited by Jean-Claud Guédon (Key Perspectives, 2004, 7). Since that date, open access journals have proliferated (see the *Directory of Open Access Journals* of Lund University Library (2004)), partly as a result of initiatives such as the Public Library of Science and PubMed Central. That these initiatives have the support of the academic community and governments is demonstrated by the UK's Joint Information Systems Committee (JISC) and the Australian Government paying to enable respectively all UK and all Australian HEIs to publish through BioMed Central (BioMed Central, 2003a, b).

Subject-based repositories have been in evidence for some years; well known examples are arXiv, for physics, and CogPrints, for cognitive sciences. Institutional repositories are, however, perhaps more interesting from the point of view of the academic librarian. One can foresee a time when every university will host its own; as they become universal they offer an alternative to publishing in commercial journals; they are hospitable to teaching materials as well as to research; finally, and more parochially, they often fall within the librarian's remit.

The institutional repository has been defined as 'a web-based database . . . of scholarly material which is institutionally defined . . .; cumulative and perpetual . . .; open and interoperable . . .; and thus collects, stores and disseminates'

(Mark Ware Consulting, 2004). Repositories started to become more widespread as storage costs decreased, open access standards became accepted, and software such as MIT's DSpace became freely available. At the start of 2004, 45 institutional repositories were identified, operating in 17 countries; 12 were in the USA, with respectable numbers in France, Germany, Italy, Sweden and the UK. Of the documents contained in them, 22% were e-prints (both pre- and post-prints), 20% theses and dissertations, and 58% other, such as reports, images or teaching materials. However, the number of documents in each repository is typically not large: among Open Access Initiative data providers, the median is 314, more than a third host fewer than 100, and more than two-thirds fewer than 1000. The main subjects covered are those already associated with pre-print archives: physics, mathematics, computer science and economics.

The institutional repositories seem currently to pose no threat to traditional commercial academic journals. The size of the individual repositories is small, the types of material hosted eclectic, the subject coverage limited. The research by Mark Ware Consulting (2004, 17) shows that, even where repositories have strong institutional backing, take-up by academics is, to say the least, patchy. Following our discussion above of the relative value of dissemination and validation, this is no surprise: academics publishing papers are following personal and institutional pressures to publish in established peer-reviewed journals. Academics seem to demonstrate a split personality. As readers (consumers or users of information), they are radical, passing motions exhorting librarians to support 'affordable scholarly journals' and refuse 'big deal' subscriptions (Stanford University, 2004). As authors, they are conservative, not supporting radical initiatives such as e-journals and institutional repositories: only a tiny proportion of editorial boards has resigned to set up alternatives. These may be the same individuals, but operating at different ends of the information chain.

According to Mark Ware Consulting (2004, 35), publishers are largely unconcerned by the advent of institutional repositories: 74% felt that the impact would be either neutral or insignificant. This is not due solely to the low levels of population of repositories: the established structures and conventions of hard copy that enable the packaging into titles and the indexing and retrieval of individual articles are at best nascent.

While this complacency may be justified on cultural grounds, it may be threatened by technical developments. It has been reported recently, for instance, that Google is to support the identification and retrieval of articles from institutional repositories (Young, 2004). It has also long been recognized (Ball, 1996, 114–15) that it would be possible to create virtual journals, where the individual articles were not brought together but remained distributed through the institutional repositories. Appropriate security and authentication would, of course, be necessary, but it is entirely possible for articles to be peer-reviewed and accepted into a journal and the articles to be identified only by the existence of the journal title in a metadata field.

The phenomenon of open access journals and institutional repositories represents a radical telescoping of the information chain: publication, aggregation and access are compressed into one link, leaving much reduced or no roles for libraries and other intermediaries.

The economics of e-journal publishing

Examining the economics of scholarly publishing is really like entering a looking-glass world, where the usual relationships of, for instance, price and sales are inverted.

Producers and consumers

One anomaly, evident particularly in journal publishing, is that the producers of the basic product – the articles that appear in journals or the conference papers – are not rewarded directly. Generally, they are ragged-gowned philanthropists, donating the fruits of their labour to the publishers. They also donate their labour as editors and peer-reviewers for little or no reward. In general, neither the institutions that employ them nor the funders of research projects seek to retain the rights in the intellectual property created. Indeed, the institutions then purchase the journals in which the articles subsequently appear. There is, therefore, a double subsidy of the publishers by the academic world. This is mitigated to an extent by the indirect financial benefits accruing to both institutions and individual academics noted above.

Another interesting characteristic of the financial side of scholarly publishing is that the user or consumer in general does not pay for the information used. A little thought shows that library fines are levied not for the information delivered but for transgressions against an institutional code; charges for photocopies are for flexibility of use, not for the actual information. Payment is made from an institutional budget, generally delegated to the librarian. The user is therefore insulated from considerations of cost and the effects of inflation: unlike most products price does not affect demand because the user is not obliged to place a value on the product consumed.

Pricing

A simple hard-copy example illustrates the effects of pricing on the market place. (An accessible treatment of the economics is given by Poynder (2002), and a fuller treatment by McCabe (2000).) If the publisher discounts the library price of a must-have journal by 50% it is most unlikely that subscriptions will double. Some libraries will take an additional copy; there will be fewer cancellations; but the number of subscriptions will not rise hugely. Instead, libraries will spend the saving on other titles, generally from other publishers. By discounting, the publisher has lost profitability and decreased market share, hardly good business. The converse is also true. If the library price of the must-have journal is doubled, some subscriptions will be lost but, since the title is must-have, by no means 50%: other journals will be cancelled instead. By raising the price, the publisher will increase profitability and market share. The disconnection, already noted above, of the user, the only true judge of value, from price paid has fed the rampant inflation seen in hard-copy journal prices.

The same commercial logic applies in electronic publishing. It makes no sense for publishers to offer discounts to the individual library, still less to the consortium. By so doing, they would simply and immediately decrease both profit and market share. Instead of lower prices publishers offer additional content. As is discussed below, this bundling puts the publisher in an even stronger position vis-à-vis libraries.

Costs

A recent study of the costs of scientific publishing shows that, as publishers have long maintained, there is little difference in costs between hard-copy and electronic publishing (Wellcome Trust, 2004, 10). Electronic journals are only slightly cheaper: there is no cost for paper, packaging or distribution, but there is a cost for maintenance and storage of the data; the editorial, marketing and fulfilment costs are the same, and constitute by far the greatest portion of the costs.

More interesting are the study's conclusions about open access journals. 'First-copy costs' (the inescapable costs of putting an article into the required form and format for publication) are the same for both open access and subscription journals. However, open access journals do not incur the costs of subscription management, licence negotiation, sales and marketing that subscription journals bear. It is estimated that the total costs per article of a good-to-high-quality subscription journal are $2750, and of a good-to-high-quality open access journal $1950 – a difference of about 30%. The difference for medium-quality journals is the same (Wellcome Trust, 2004, 35) – $1425 for a subscription journal and $1025 for open access journals.

These costs are considerable, and must be borne by someone. Until now, the costs have been borne generally by individuals and organizations contributing time and resources to prove the concept. However, for open access journals to be a serious alternative to subscription journals, their financial basis must be sound. The model most likely to be adopted is that the author (or their institution or research funder) should pay. Payment would be made firstly for submission of an article to the peer-review process (the Wellcome Trust report suggests a fee of $175), and secondly for actual publication of the successful articles. The high-quality journals will, of course, reject more submissions than the medium-quality journals; these submission fees will form a large proportion of the first-copy costs. Medium-quality journals will reject fewer submissions, and may well therefore charge the individual author more for actual publication. (The Wellcome Trust report posits publication costs to the author of $675 for medium-quality journals and $550 for high-quality journals.)

Implications for the library of this model have yet to be fully appreciated. If open access journals become widespread, there will be a fall in subscriptions paid by libraries. However, there will be cost increases elsewhere. Although commercial publishers may bring out fewer titles and sell fewer subscriptions, their overhead costs will remain the same: prices will therefore rise. Universities, rather than individual authors, would, in all probability, bear the costs of submission to open access journals. A decrease in the subscription bill paid by libraries may therefore be matched by a decrease in the available funds.

Interestingly, under this model institutions undertaking little research stand to benefit, since the costs of journal production will be borne by institutions with large research outputs. This is just in one sense: the beneficiaries of the process of validation and subsequent publication bear the costs. In another sense, it is unjust: the beneficiaries of the process of dissemination pay nothing.

E-books

Although revolutionary in terms of delivery, the advent of e-journals has not changed the mode of use. Indexes and abstracts are searched; articles are selected; prints of them are procured. This is fundamentally no different from the hard-copy process of getting photocopies of articles, either from one's own library or on interlibrary loan, after a literature search. The process has been telescoped by the technology, and the user is more in control; but the end-product is the same and this is essentially the way that scholars have worked for many years.

However, e-books are different, partly because of the extent of their individual content. Library users are either tied to a screen to read large volumes of text, or obliged to print it themselves. This is not the way that users, or librarians, have worked with hard-copy books, and the end-product is quite different. The difference is magnified because the numbers making intensive use of e-books, particularly textbooks, comprising the whole undergraduate population, are much larger than the numbers making intensive use of e-journals. Cultural and technical difficulties (network and hardware availability, printing capacities and costs) are potentially much more critical.

E-books can take a number of forms. Initially they were intended to be read on dedicated hardware devices. However uptake outside North America was very slow, because of cost, lack of available hardware, and poor on-screen readability. The norm now, particularly in HE, is for a software solution (such as Adobe) run on a PC, laptop or personal digital assistant (PDA). Given their portability and multiple functionality, the last two devices seem destined to push out the dedicated reader. For current purposes, we shall concentrate on networked or networkable e-books, made available through PCs or laptops.

Approaches to e-books in terms of functionality are dominated by the metaphor of the book and the database. Gibbons, Peters and Bryan (2003, 6–22) define seven types of functionality, of which six fit the prevailaing metaphor:

- physical functionality of the device (such as readability, ergonomics)
- functionality that helps read the content (such as searchability, navigational tools)
- enhancing functionality (such as inclusion of multimedia, links to data and bulletin boards)
- functionality that places the content in a context (such as links to other e-content, inter-textual searchability)
- functionality that helps the reader 'possess' the text (such as making annotations, printing)
- functionality that supports library activities (such as preserving the confidentiality of users, being 'scrubbable').

The supply chain

Librarians know how to buy hard-copy books; publishers and intermediaries know how to sell them. The channels and roles of the participants in the supply chain are well established. Perhaps the most interesting characteristics of the supply chain for e-books are fluidity and uncertainty: what is available to be bought, on what terms and from whom.

Authors are generally in favour of the alternative medium, since it offers the possibility of additional royalties. However, concerns have been voiced about the ease of plagiarism in the electronic format.

One potential although seldom realized benefit, for the user and library, of the electronic medium is greatly enhanced granularity: it should be possible to subscribe to content at the level of the article, the chapter, even the page. Authors may see this as a threat to the assertion of their moral rights, and also to their royalties if only segments of a book are bought instead of the complete package.

The involvement of aggregators is quite confused. In North America, traditional wholesalers such as Barnes & Noble have entered the market; new players have also emerged, such as Overdrive and Lightning Source, offering digital content warehouses. They may offer additional services such as digitization. Online retailers, such as Amazon and Swotbooks, are selling e-books direct to the public. As far as library supply is concerned, new aggregators have emerged, such as NetLibrary and ebrary. Some traditional library suppliers are also acting as agents for them or wholesalers or publishers. Suppliers of virtual learning environments (VLEs), such as Blackboard, are offering e-books, sometimes in very small chunks, for integration with course-ware produced in house.

Librarians generally welcome e-books and are keen to integrate them into their collections, if the price is affordable. One of the main applications foreseen for e-books is to replace the hard-copy textbook that is in high demand. E-books are thus seen as the equivalent of the hard-copy short-loan collection, which has loan periods of only a few hours or overnight. E-books, of course, have the major advantage of eliminating the intense but repetitive labour of issuing and re-shelving large volumes of stock, as well as of accessioning, repairing and withdrawing them; they are also available 24x7 and to students remote from the campus, and can be integrated into VLEs (Armstrong and Lonsdale, 2003, 7).

Academic staff seem more reluctant to adopt them, let alone champion them. This is partly due to fears of increased plagiarism, facilitated by the electronic medium. It is also due to the fact that publishers do not seem to push e-books as an alternative to hard copy, or even advertise their existence. Given the economics outlined below this is hardly surprising. However, since academics are the main engine for the prescription and hence acquisition of book-stock, their lack of engagement will act as a brake on the uptake and availability of e-books.

As discussed above, e-books have the potential to replace the physical short-loan collection. If they do so successfully, this may have the effect of decreasing the sale of textbooks to students. Education for Change, University of Stirling Centre for Publishing Studies and University of Stirling Information Services (2003, 63) point out that, because libraries account for only a small percentage of textbook sales, 'loss of as little as 10% of printed textbook sales to students would require a doubling of income from libraries to maintain the same revenue to publishers overall'. Library budgets may, therefore, become the victims of the success of the medium, as publishers increase the price of electronic textbooks to compensate for loss of revenue from students.

Physical realization of a title now occurs at the end of the chain. Indeed, it may not happen at all, but in practice substantial portions of titles will be printed by each serious user. The cost is not included in the price of the e-book, but must be borne by either the user or the university. To an extent this cost for the user will be offset by what might have been spent photocopying a printed version.

One encouraging trend for libraries is the unheralded advent of what one may call open access e-books. Much grey literature, notoriously slow and difficult to source in hard copy, is now freely available on the websites of the originators. This is particularly the case with government and official and other public bodies and organizations. A glance at the bibliography at the end of this volume demonstrates how prevalent, and how useful, this phenomenon is. There are obvious advantages, in terms of ease and immediacy of obtaining the texts. There are problems too, particularly the permanence and continuing availability of the texts and the websites.

Currently the business models for e-books are dominated by the traditional structures of book-buying. But this may well change. Will we see the development of subject consortia of academic departments from several institutions, which act as both producers and purchasers of academic texts? Will new e-only publishers arise, perhaps within HE itself, perhaps within the media, commissioning and producing learning packages designed for delivery through VLEs? Will universities defray the increased costs of e-books by passing some of them on to students, using micro-charging through credit or smart cards to act as collectors of revenue for the publishers in place of bookshops? The fluidity of the supply chain for e-books opens up the possibility of these and other new business models.

Conclusion

This chapter has discussed some of the underlying structures and economics of the information chain, highlighting the differences between hard-copy and electronic publication. The next chapters have a more practical emphasis, examining the commercial relationships between links in the information chain and outlining strategies and techniques for managing these relationships.

3
Relationships with suppliers

Introduction

In the 1970s it was commonplace for the larger libraries to be almost completely self-sufficient. The processes associated with selection, ordering, cataloguing, classification and processing of books were all handled in-house. Circulation of stock was achieved by large numbers of clerical staff, as was maintenance of card, sheaf and guard-book catalogues. The larger libraries had in-house binderies.

Over the past 30 years, the landscape has changed. The advent of e-resources is an obvious difference: now a large portion of current journal stock will be held by external agencies. Equally, many of the repetitive processes associated with hard-copy stock have also been farmed out to suppliers, who offer benefits deriving from economies of scale and specialization. To achieve these benefits, libraries have had to open up their systems, processes and procedures to suppliers, bringing about a fundamental change in relationships. Libraries are contracting in both senses: they carry out fewer functions (such as binding) in-house; they also rely more and more on relationships with suppliers that are governed by contracts.

This chapter examines the relationships with suppliers of:

- hard-copy materials
- electronic resources
- library management systems
- virtual learning environments.

Suppliers of hard-copy materials

The start of the acquisition process is book selection. Particularly in the academic library, this is viewed as a core professional task, since stock is so closely identified with learning, teaching and research. If a lecturer recommends that 200 students read chapters six to ten of Jones's book on macroeconomics, there is no point in having only Smith's book, no matter how good it may be. The library would also be failing in its duty to support teaching if it acquired only one copy of Jones, and placed it on long loan. Subject or faculty librarians pride themselves on their integration into the academic and research processes, not only providing recommended texts, but also developing collections in line with academic programmes and research, discovering and evaluating new resources and alerting academic staff. (Dale, Holland and Matthews (2005) give a full treatment of the role of the subject librarian and integration with the academic process.)

Supplier selection
Public libraries

Entrusting book selection to suppliers may therefore seem to subject librarians an abdication of a core responsibility. It has, however, been tried with some success in public libraries. Capital Planning Information (1999, 13, 33) identified the possible benefits to public libraries as: release of staff for other stock management; wider range of publishers and titles supplied, because of suppliers' specialist knowledge; supply of books at publication date. The study demonstrated that supplier selection was practicable and achieved most of these benefits. Fundamental to success is the development both of detailed stock management and selection policies by libraries and of partnerships with suppliers based on respect, understanding and the open exchange of information.

One of the best known examples of supplier selection occurred in Liverpool Libraries and Information Services (Naylor, 2000). Here the impetus was the introduction of 'best value', which necessitated a response to a steady decline in the number of book issues. Supplier selection was introduced for all new books, with library staff themselves selecting for the maintenance of core stock. This division was felt to reflect the knowledge and expertise of both sides of the supply equation. It was recognized that the choice of titles selected by the suppliers could only be as good as the specification of requirements by Liverpool. Much effort was invested in the latter, which reached its 17th edition within a year. The chosen suppliers were closely involved throughout the process of developing the concept and service, visiting libraries and advising on specifications.

It seems that Liverpool has benefited from supplier selection, particularly in terms of the range of stock available in libraries, speed of supply and saving in staff time. However, some caution remains, for instance about the range of non-fiction publishers supplied. There is a fear that the stock of the libraries will come to mirror that of the popular high street bookshop, and large proportions of the non-fiction book-fund, especially for the more academic areas covered by the large central reference library, are still spent by library staff. There is some evidence to support this fear of homogeneity: Chapman and Spiller (2000, 22) distinguish a trend towards public libraries spending a much smaller proportion of book-funds on material more than a year old, and attribute this in part at least to the effect of supplier selection.

Supplier selection seems at best patchy still in public libraries, mostly evident on the small scale, for instance for popular fiction authors or to stock a new library, rather than on the large scale tried by Liverpool. One inhibitor identified by Muir and Fishwick (2000, 12–13) is the lack of data and information about the populations served by public libraries: without such information it is impossible to write a proper specification for the service.

The Liverpool experience demonstrates the importance of the specification, both for tendering and for monitoring the service provided. It also highlights that the relationship with suppliers needs to be one of partnership rather than opposition.

Academic libraries

The misgivings about supplier selection in the public library sector have no doubt reinforced the reluctance of academic librarians to experiment with it. Supplier selection is, however, widespread in academic libraries in North America, where it masquerades, rather misleadingly, under the title of 'approval plans'. In the most complete form of the approval plan, the library specifies the material it wishes to purchase (which may be by subject, geographic area, publisher, etc.) and sets budgetary limits; the vendor supplies material meeting the specification without further intervention by the library. A halfway house is the 'slip plan': the supplier sends notifications of titles meeting the specification (generally electronically) to designated library staff, who initiate the selection and ordering process.

The US survey by Brown and Forsyth (1999, 232) shows five major vendors supplying 291 academic libraries with significant approval plans. The marketplace seems stable, with half the responding libraries having the same supplier(s) for more than four years; over 61% used one or two suppliers only.

The marketplace does, however, show a trend towards consolidation: a previous survey 15 years earlier (Reidelbach and Shirk, 1984, 158–9) shows eight vendors rather than five.

This is not surprising. Approval plans entail major continuing investment in both systems and staff by suppliers, and are complex to manage and implement for both libraries and suppliers alike, since they mesh with so many library operations and departments. Brown and Forsyth (1999, 253) note that libraries rank 'corporate reputation and business practice' as the third most important factor in selecting approval plan vendors, close behind technical performance measures. This is a reflection of concern about the long-term viability of companies that become an integral element of library processes, requiring stable relationships. The adoption of approval plans will, therefore, emphasize the trend towards increasing dominance of the market by large suppliers and lack of movement by libraries between suppliers.

Benefits

As we have seen, approval plans are widespread in North America, and there are major benefits for the library, if the plans work well. The amount of staff time spent on the selection process is greatly reduced: the supplier's staff and systems do the work previously duplicated across many libraries. Suppliers are able to offer higher discounts because the terms on which they trade with publishers are more favourable: instead of ordering single copies of individual titles piecemeal against firm orders, they are able to order once in bulk to satisfy all approval plans.

In addition, the way in which the suppliers work, profiling books for approval plans only when they are published, brings benefits. The traditional method of libraries entering firm orders for titles often means that books are ordered before they are published, or even before they are written: librarians and academics work from publishers' advance notices of books in press. The approval plan has the effect of shortening the average time of supply, measured from date of order to date of receipt in the library. It also means that libraries make much more effective use of their institutions' money: it is spent on books that come into stock almost immediately, instead of lying fallow, committed to purchase of materials not yet, or even never to be, produced. There is the added efficiency gain of not having to administer committed but unspent funds, or to cancel unfulfilled orders.

There is also some evidence that approval plans work well for specialist collections or libraries. Jenkins (2003, 180) maintains that approval plans identify publications in disciplines, such as nursing and education, not adequately covered by traditional selection and reviewing tools. The experience of the College of Mount St Joseph Library shows that the approval plan doubled the number of titles acquired for four vocational disciplines within a year. Brown and Forsyth (1999, 259) report that, while approval plans traditionally have been considered ideal for larger libraries, smaller libraries with budgets of less than $100,000 found that approval plans served them well too.

Concerns

There are also, of course, concerns about the effects of approval plans. Only the large suppliers can afford to develop and implement them. They therefore become yet another barrier to competition, tending to keep the smaller suppliers out of the marketplace. They also mean that libraries become even more dependent on their suppliers. This combination, of increasing reliance on suppliers and a marketplace that is open to less and less competition, may be dangerous for libraries in the longer term.

Professional concerns are evident too. Supplier selection, or the approval plan, introduces another filter between publisher and library as customer. Willett (1998) makes the case that the alternative press does not figure in supplier-selected materials; reliance on suppliers could therefore tend to homogenize collections and accentuate the dominance of established publishers. This does indeed raise what must be an underlying concern. How do the suppliers pre-select books or publishers for inclusion in plans? However, this has always been a problem with selection aids used by librarians and academics. How, for instance, do journal publishers select books for review? Taking an approval plan does not necessarily imply the dormancy of professional awareness, or the absence of pressure on suppliers to meet libraries' requirements. Nor does it imply sole sourcing: it can indeed be argued that the approval plan frees staff time to concentrate on the esoteric, the out-of-the-way, the hard-to-source publications.

Perhaps a more fundamental concern is raised by Gasson's report of his interview with Philip Blackwell (2002, 22). In the context of discussing the level of discount allowed by publishers to booksellers, Gasson notes the power of library suppliers to influence book sales. Philip Blackwell comments: 'we profile over 40,000 titles a year for targeted approval plans . . . and that definitely drives sales. Does the margin we are given [by publishers] really reflect the investment that we have made to sell those books?' The profiling book supplier has three options to recoup the investment: bargain with the publisher for a bigger discount; pass the cost to the library, and become less competitive; or stop profiling the publisher. For librarians this is a sobering reminder that suppliers are commercial entities, driven by the bottom line. When entering and monitoring contracts with suppliers, librarians need a high level of commercial awareness in order to reconcile the supplier's concern for the bottom line with the interests of the library's users.

Shelf-ready materials

While supplier selection may seem somewhat controversial outside North America, there is growing acceptance and implementation of the shelf-ready book. Suppliers have for many years carried out the physical processing of books, adding, for instance, date labels, ownership stamps and security tags. Now more and more libraries are outsourcing cataloguing and classification to their suppliers too: files of data are sent to the library, generally by electronic data interchange (EDI) when books are despatched from the supplier's warehouse, and are uploaded into the library management system (LMS). Quality checks are carried out on both the data and the standards of cataloguing, classification and physical processing of the books; otherwise the books are sent straight to the shelf on unpacking.

An early academic experimenter in the UK was the University of Huddersfield, which found considerable savings in the cost of acquisition and cataloguing, and in through-put time (Weaver et al., 1999, 29–30). Staff also compared classification numbers and subject indexing supplied with that done in-house, and found external supply to be satisfactory.

The trend towards shelf-ready books has been intensified by the regional purchasing consortia, which since the late 1990s have required provision of a full shelf-ready service from their book suppliers. More and more libraries are obtaining at least a part of their stock shelf-ready, particularly those with large book-funds, which tend in the UK to be the newer universities with their emphasis on teaching.

There are obvious advantages and attractions in this development. What is, *pace* the cataloguers, in the majority of cases a repetitive and fairly undemanding process is completely farmed out to the supplier. Both professional and paraprofessional staff are freed for other, more user-oriented work. The backlogs that accumulate so easily in cataloguing departments, because staff resources are limited and unable to cope with the peaks of new acquisition, are eliminated: suppliers operate with much larger pools of staff, geared to high volumes, that tend to obviate peaks and troughs. The time elapsing between an order being placed and the book being available to the user is much reduced.

Elements of the shelf-ready process may, however, be problematic. To achieve cost savings, libraries must use standard classification schemes and cataloguing practices. Suppliers may accommodate the application of optional elements within the current edition of, say, Dewey, but will understandably charge for eccentric elements, common in many libraries, such as the use in particular subject areas of an earlier edition of Dewey or of a classification scheme developed in-house.

Another service, which is as yet fairly uncommon, is the shelf-ready serial. Most of the serials agents offer a 'consolidated' service. This was generally developed to decrease the costs for libraries of procuring serials from abroad: individual issues of different serials are consolidated by the agent into a single shipment from the country of publication, thus saving freight costs. However, the agents will also process the serial parts using stationery supplied by the library, and supply check-in data that can be uploaded into the LMS. Taken together these elements, originally developed for the supply of serials from abroad, constitute a shelf-ready service.

Lessons

There is a readily identifiable trend towards libraries contracting out more and more processes once regarded as core professional practice. (For a full discussion of the implications, see Chapter 5.) In some areas, such as supplier selection or classification, librarians may feel that they are surrendering too much control over professional standards to a commercial supplier, and that service to the user may be reduced, as for instance classification becomes inconsistent with former in-house practice. There is also a perceived danger, common with any form of outsourcing, of becoming too reliant on external agencies. Suppliers do go bankrupt; ownership may change: what are the effects then on a core element of library operations?

Against these fears must be set the clear advantage of being able to divert staff time from repetitive processes to service that is focused on the user and the particular demands of the library's clientele. All librarians should question the opportunity cost of continuing to select, catalogue and process books and serials in-house, when suppliers will do it more efficiently.

The benefits can be achieved only by working in close partnership with suppliers, on a basis of trust and openness. There has to be substantial investment on both sides, at least of staff resources. For the benefit of both sides, the relationship has to be based on clear, full specifications of the services to be provided and on clear contractual arrangements. Because of the substantial investment required of suppliers, and of the integration of suppliers into library systems and processes, there is a trend towards long-term relationships with a few large suppliers.

Suppliers of electronic resources

Chapter 2 notes a major difference between hard-copy and electronic resources: the shift from product to service. Having bought a physical product, the hard-copy book or journal, libraries can do with it as they will, as long as intellectual property rights are not infringed. They can keep it for 500 years, or throw it away; they can lend it to staff, students, external borrowers or another library; they can transfer it to a partner college or sell it. However, generally libraries do not buy electronic resources outright: they buy access to them – a service not a product.

Licence constraints

The conditions of access to any commercially provided information resource are tightly controlled by a licence, which will specify how long the access will last, where the resource may be used, by whom and for what purposes. Libraries now buy access to many different resources from many different providers. Each provider may well have its own form of licence, which of course brings challenges for both library staff and users. However, in the UK, many resources will be bought under arrangements made by NESLI or Eduserv/CHEST; these are covered by standard licences, developed to reflect the activity of the sector while recognizing the interests of the publisher.

The standard Eduserv licence (Eduserv, 2004) covers usage for the normal business of a university, taken to include 'teaching; research; personal educational development; administration and the management of the Licensee's organization; development work associated with any of the above'. Specifically excluded are 'consultancy or services leading to commercial exploitation of Product; work of significant benefit to the employer of students on industrial placement or part-time courses'. Generally, remote access, whether by distance learners or others, is permitted. However, use by retired members of staff, alumni and walk-in users (i.e. anyone not belonging to the institution) is not allowed (Eduserv, 2003).

Many resources are of course not available under standard licences; the terms of these individual licences may restrict use even more. Librarians need to be alive to these restrictions and negotiate appropriate access, for instance for the distance learner, whether studying at a FEC or simply remote from the university's campus.

Licences add to the complexity of provision today. It is clear from the discussion of the HE context in Chapter 1 that it is commonplace for universities to enter many different types of relationship with other institutions. These relationships may spring from the core business of teaching: universities are encouraged to sub-contract the teaching of courses to FECs (often misleadingly known as franchise courses – see Chapter 6 for a full discussion); they validate the HE courses of institutions without degree-awarding powers; they franchise their courses to commercially run colleges. Other activities, arising from research and knowledge transfer, seek to generate income: consultancy, applied research leading to product development, teaching company schemes. These activities are also encouraged as part of HE's mission to power business through knowledge transfer. Many university libraries also offer subscription membership to local companies and institutions, helping to fulfil the requirement of universities to engage with the local community.

Many of the latter activities involving relationships with the commercial world may not be covered by the standard licence (which excludes, for instance, consultancy). It is also not clear that students on courses validated by a university, although technically registered as its students, are eligible to access resources under the standard licence.

As with all contracts there are some fine judgements and interpretations to be made. One rule of thumb is to consider the direction in which money flows in any relationship. If the university is paid for an activity, such as consultancy or validation, the use of the licensed resources is suspect: the university can be seen to be selling on the resources as part of a service, and the publisher has potentially lost a sale. However, if the university pays another institution, such as a FEC teaching its courses, use of the resources is allowed.

The big deal

Another major difference between hard-copy and electronic resources is that libraries are more often dealing directly with publishers rather than intermediaries. If one does not like the service or prices offered by an intermediary or aggregator, such as a bookseller, one can move business to a competitor. The purchasing consortia have been particularly successful in exploiting this competition. Booksellers, for instance, are keen to increase their share of the market at the expense of their competitors. They have therefore been willing to offer high discounts to consortia to achieve this; the discounts are a portion of the margin offered by the publisher to the bookseller.

As noted in Chapter 2, publishers, on the other hand, are monopolists: only they own the rights to their content and determine the terms. In the environment of consumer publications, there is some substitutability: instead of buying *The Times* one can buy *The Independent*; they are different brands but with very similar news content. However, in the academic world there is virtually no substitutability of primary content: if researchers in an academic department's specialism publish in *Journal A* and *Journal B*, *Journal X* and *Journal Y* are of no interest.

Chapter 2 demonstrates that it makes no economic sense for publishers to discount to the library sector: they simply lose profitability and market share as savings are spent elsewhere. So instead of discounts, they have offered electronic access to additional content in the form of the so-called big, or all-you-can-eat, deal. This is particularly prevalent in the field of e-journals, but may also be seen in the field of e-books.

Presumed benefits

Under the big deal, a journal publisher will grant access to all content for three or five years. There is an annual subscription, often based on and higher than the cost of the subscriber's previous print subscriptions, with some built-in increase for inflation and generally a no-cancellation clause. Libraries and their users will therefore have access to all of the publisher's content spanning however many years are available in the electronic archive.

There are potential benefits for both sides. Users have immediate access to material previously not subscribed to, at no incremental cost. Libraries can predict inflation over the term of the agreement, and save money from the interlibrary loans budget. Publishers have a stable revenue stream for a number of years, with no cancellations.

But things are seldom as straightforward as they seem. There is some statistical evidence to show that users are downloading or hitting articles well outside the range of the previously subscribed core of hard-copy titles. Understandably, this has caused librarians a fair amount of anguish, since it implies that their past collecting policy has been ill advised. However, one has to treat this evidence with some caution. It has not been collected for very long: it offers a short time-series at the start of a new service. There is no real comparison with previous data: librarians have generally not collected usage data for their hard-copy journals, partly because much consultation of them has been within the library. There is also the sweet-shop syndrome: children suddenly given the freedom of a sweet shop will gorge initially far beyond the value of their pocket money before their appetite stabilizes. The take-up of articles by academics may decline too over time as the novelty disappears. Also, we may be observing the substitution of full article hits or downloads for previous use of abstracting services: because the download or consultation is free, academics may use that mechanism where they would previously have been satisfied with an abstract. In other words the distortion noted in Chapter 2, arising from the divorce of the user from the cost of the information, is magnified.

The prima facie case that the big deal offers major benefits in terms of access to information is not necessarily proved; indeed there is some countervailing statistical evidence. Hamaker (2003), for instance, notes that 28% of *Science Direct* titles accounted for 75% of downloads at the University of North Carolina; 34% of titles had five downloads or fewer; 40% of usage occurred in a single month for 57% of titles. Nicholas and Huntington's pilot study of the Emerald big deal (2002, 149, 151) shows that 45% of subscribers viewed only one journal out of 118; another 40% viewed between two and five journals. So 85% of subscribers viewed less than 5% of the available titles. 44% of subscribers viewed only one subject area out of about ten; a further 19% viewed only two subject areas. The core collection, it seems, is still alive and well, and only camouflaged by the big deal.

Challenges

There is a hidden danger in the apparent benefit of the full output of some of the bigger publishers being made available through libraries. Guédon (2001, 24) traces the influence of the citation indexes' documentation of impact factors for journals in creating a core collection of must-have journals for particular disciplines. He also posits an increase in citations of the journals of big deal publishers (understandable given their availability) in the research output of subscribing universities. There is, therefore, potentially a vicious circle, where the journals in big deals have higher and higher impact factors, to the detriment of journals outside the big deals. The effect on the marketplace will be to undermine the financial viability of such journals and their (generally smaller) publishers.

The big deal is also challenging for librarians. Under it, libraries no longer take the decisions on developing collections that they have been used to: they will increasingly decide on content not at the journal level but at the publisher level. This is a qualitative change and one that does not necessarily work in the favour of libraries and their users. The user is focused on the article, to a lesser extent on the journal title, and most certainly not on the publisher. In the electronic environment, where the physical package – the title – is no longer necessary for purchase, the aim of libraries and users surely should be to increase the granularity of decision making, not decrease it.

The big deal may presage a further unwelcome effect on the marketplace. It commits a library to either buy or cancel the entire content of a monopolist: the monopoly is thereby intensified. The monopoly is intensified even further in the case of national deals covering an entire library sector such as HE. Such intensification cannot be in the interests of the purchaser.

There is also a danger that, at renewal time, publishers can offer libraries a stark choice: pay an additional 50% (or more) for the big deal or cancel. Few academic libraries will be able to refuse the big deals, because they contain so many must-have titles. The inflation apparent with hard-copy titles, enabled by the disconnection of user from price paid, will now be further fuelled by bundling into the big deal. The consequence will therefore be that journals outside the big deals will be cancelled. Publishers, particularly the smaller ones will cease trading, and there will be further consolidation in the market.

E-books

Until now, this section has focused on e-journals, which consume a large and growing portion of library budgets. E-books, which are becoming more and more important, offer some interesting similarities with and differences from e-journals.

The technology offers the possibility of greatly enhanced granularity, allowing subscription at the level not of the title but of the chapter or even page. Generally this is not yet happening. Indeed there is a tendency to bundling, either the whole of an aggregator's offering or discrete libraries of several hundred or a thousand texts. This is generally disliked by librarians, for the same reasons cited above for e-journals. However, one aggregator does allow libraries to change the titles subscribed to month by month.

E-books are generally more expensive than their printed equivalents, as are e-journals. As the section in Chapter 2 on business models for e-books points out, this difference will increase if sales to students of hard copy textbooks decline. However, large-scale adoption by libraries to replace short loan collections and other heavily used texts offers the prospect of substantial savings in particularly labour-intensive areas. These savings of staff costs may well be greater than with e-journals.

One important difference from printed books for the library is that the cost of e-books tends to be recurrent (annual subscription to a service) rather than one-off. The implications of this shift have not yet been fully recognized. As e-books proliferate and if subscription remains the predominant model, less and less of libraries' spending will be discretionary. Spending on hard copy will suffer, as spending on monographs has suffered during times of high inflation in journal prices. The big publishers, with bundled deals, will gain.

Business models tend to be linked to or indeed mimic hard-copy business models. NetLibrary, for instance, currently charges for each title a one-time licence fee, roughly the published price for hard copy, plus an annual access fee of 15%, or a fee of 55% for permanent access. The base cost of owning an e-book for five years is 155% of the hard-copy price. Since most UK university libraries are members of purchasing consortia, they gain substantial discounts on hard-copy prices. Depending on the level of discount, the premium on owning an e-book for five years can therefore be between 70% and 90% on top of the price paid for the hard-copy equivalent.

Other aggregators offer only bundles. Some prices can be advantageous, if all or the majority of the titles would have been bought anyway. Other prices are not so advantageous. One aggregator offers 2600 titles at a cost of $32,000 per annum; over five years the cost is $160,000. Assuming a shelf-life of five years for an academic title, and an average cost of $50 per title, 3200 hard-copy volumes could be bought for the price of 2600 in electronic form. Given, indeed, that a fair proportion of these titles would not have been bought in hard copy, the pricing is certainly not advantageous to the library.

In the UK, value added tax (VAT) is a distorting factor. It is charged at 0% on hard-copy books and journals, but at the standard rate of 17.5% on electronic materials. It should be possible to make some savings in resource, distribution and production costs if selling electronic texts. However, if publishers are to match the actual hard-copy price paid by a library or end-user, they have to absorb the differential created by VAT, while still offering intermediaries a margin similar to that of the hard-copy retailer. According to models using this assumption developed for Education for Change (2003, 81–4), print-only publication of textbooks is more profitable for publishers over a period of six years than electronic-only publication, or parallel publication with significant migration to e-book purchasing.

Lessons

E-resources offer many benefits for librarian and user, notably flexibility and access from anywhere at any time. However, they can also be problematic. Licences bring constraints unknown with hard copy. There are real threats, not only to library budgets, but also to the continued existence of journals and smaller publishers. The technology offers the possibility of subscription or purchase at the level of the article or chapter, a degree of granularity that matches the way the resources are used. However, in many cases publishers have taken control of the business models, subverting this possibility and forcing libraries to buy in huge bundles. Given their position as monopolists, it is difficult to wrest this control from them; the next chapter offers some strategies and techniques.

Suppliers of library management systems

Apart from buildings, the library management system (LMS) is probably the most expensive investment a library will make. Breeding (2004, 22) estimates that over the first ten years of its life, an LMS will typically cost the library $776,000, or nearly $78,000 per year. Generally, this sum is made up of an initial capital cost for the software licence and thereafter annual maintenance charges of 10–20% of the initial cost.

There are a number of mature LMSs for the large library, some with a development history of 20 years. All have the traditional core functionality for acquiring and managing hard-copy materials, and for managing borrowers. This core functionality generally extends to communication between library and book supplier for ordering; the mechanism for supporting the purchase of shelf-ready books and serials generally exists, but may need some technical customization.

Managing, and providing access to, electronic resources is, however, another matter. Traditional LMS catalogues function at the title level, for both books and serials; however, users require access to e-journals at the article level, and increasingly to e-books at the chapter level. The user will therefore search one or a number of bibliographic databases, and expect to link directly to an electronic copy or to holdings information for hard copy. There is no difference in the fundamental approach of using secondary sources to point to hard-copy primary sources; however, there is a major difference in the expectation of seamless linking between these sources from a single desktop PC. The LMS is therefore expected to interface with, or provide, link resolvers that take the user to the appropriate copy of an article (i.e. one to which the library subscribes).

E-resources are administratively much more complex than their hard-copy equivalents. Typically, as has already been discussed, usage is governed by licences, limiting such matters as period of access, number of simultaneous users, whether remote access is allowed, classes of user covered, subscription terms. While LMSs may generally have the detailed functionality for managing print subscriptions (check-in, prediction patterns, claiming missing issues, etc.), they are generally not as yet fully hospitable to electronic resource management. Given the number and complexity of individual licence agreements a single library may enter, a system of electronic resource management is becoming essential.

Also essential in the modern environment of electronically held records and data interchange is the facility for the LMS to operate successfully with other systems, such as student records, accounts and electronic payment. Other targets for integration are the managed and virtual learning environments. Over the next five to ten years, all universities will implement these environments; the standard LMS, if still in use, will need to exchange information on resources and borrowers with these environments, as well as with student record systems.

The architecture for this interoperability has still to be developed. Will the LMS evolve to provide the functionality required for the future? Or will the LMS wither, dealing only with a shrinking legacy of hard-copy books and serials, while new systems are developed to manage and link electronic resources?

As custodians of the resources and the systems that enable their exploitation, libraries need to influence as far as possible the development of systems and ensure their interoperability, whether managing books or serials, hard-copy or electronic resources, whether they are internal to the university or run by suppliers or intermediaries.

Suppliers of virtual and managed learning environments

Neither the concept nor the underlying technology of virtual learning environments (VLEs) is new, having their roots in computer-based learning materials. A VLE is defined by JISC (2000) as referring to the components of a system 'in which learners and tutors participate in on-line interactions of various kinds, including on-line learning'. Common features of a VLE include:

- controlled access to a curriculum that has been mapped to elements that can be separately assessed and recorded
- tracking student activity and achievement against these elements
- support of online learning, including access to learning resources, assessment and guidance
- communication between the learner, the tutor and other learning support specialists
- links to other administrative systems, both in-house and externally (Porter, 2002).

Typically, a lecturer will assemble a collection of information resources; these may be produced in-house, such as lecture notes, videos of lectures; they may also be hard-copy or electronic resources available through the library, or links to resources and websites held elsewhere. There will also be assessment and tracking mechanisms and the means for students to communicate with lecturers and their peers (e-mail, bulletin boards, chat facilities). The student logs into their personal VLE account on the university's web server through a standard web browser, and interacts with the materials and the lecturer. The VLE will record data about how each student is using the system.

The term 'managed learning environment' (MLE) refers to the VLE and all the administrative and information systems and processes of the university, including student records, the LMS, etc.

There are a number of suppliers of VLEs, some offering free or open source software. The two commercial leaders in HE are Blackboard and WebCT, both of which promise a degree of integration between their products and the LMS. Some suppliers also offer access to published material.

Clearly, there are challenges here. University librarians will want to integrate library resources as seamlessly as possible into the local VLE, with the minimum number of clicks; they will also want to ensure that data are exchanged between LMS and VLE. This again demonstrates the importance of the interaction between systems and of the three-way relationships between libraries and suppliers of both systems and resources.

Conclusion

It is clear that suppliers are undertaking more and more tasks traditionally carried out in-house. Fundamental to reaping the benefits from this trend and to ensuring quality of service, are partnerships with suppliers, based on a good specification and tight contract management. While electronic resources bring great benefits, they also bring risks for libraries that are difficult to manage. The complexity of the systems environment and architecture is increasing. Chapter 4 discusses in detail the strategies and techniques for managing suppliers and the market.

4
Strategies and techniques for managing suppliers

Introduction

Chapter 3 demonstrates some of the complexities of relationships with suppliers. Publishers in particular are in a powerful position vis-à-vis their customers, libraries; they are introducing business models that seem to benefit the user but are potentially dangerous in their effects, threatening the viability of the smaller publishers and exacerbating the tendency to consolidation. This chapter discusses the measures that libraries can take to strengthen their position and as far as possible take control of relationships with publishers and other suppliers.

The procurement cycle

The standard procurement cycle comprises, briefly, the following five elements: identifying the need, preparing the specification, finding the supplier, awarding the contract, and measuring and monitoring performance. Following and understanding this cycle is fundamental to taking control of relationships with suppliers and of the marketplace.

Identifying the need

The first step is to determine precisely what is required, and on what basis it should be procured – bought, leased, hired, shared. With hard-copy information, the emphasis is on buying and servicing the physical product. With electronic information, libraries are generally buying a service not a product: the emphasis is on access and the terms that govern it. Library management systems have generally been leased and then managed by individual libraries. However, recent years have seen the LMS suppliers offering more and more services, such as facilities management, and some instances of libraries joining together to procure the same system (as in the case of the University of Wales) or indeed a shared system (the University of Edinburgh and the National Library of Scotland).

It should be noted that, in much procurement for libraries, the users are not consulted directly about their needs: the budget-holders, librarians, act as proxies. This may lead to a concentration on the technical issues that affect the library, such as processing of books or EDI, rather than on those that directly affect the user, such as the functionality of e-book offerings.

Preparing the specification

Once the need has been identified, it has to be expressed in a specification. This specification is fundamental to any procurement: it informs potential suppliers of what is required, how, when and to what standards. If the specification is wrong, there is no chance of satisfying adequately the procurement needs. It should contain enough information and detail to ensure that both suppliers and purchasers are addressing the same requirement, and that suppliers can cost fully the products or services required. However, except for technical compatibility, it should not be so overly specific, for instance in detailing procedures, that it prevents negotiation or discourages suppliers from proposing innovative solutions. Suppliers know their own business better than librarians do; over-specifying stifles creativity and the development of partnership, and hence decreases the potential benefits of any procurement.

It is important that the specification should also promote open and fair competition. It should not discriminate, explicitly or implicitly, against particular suppliers or products. For instance, it may be superficially attractive to prefer local suppliers. However, a relatively distant supplier that can meet the requirements (such as next-day delivery, response times) may in fact offer a higher-quality service or a better price than the local supplier. A supplier should be judged on performance against the specification, not on the purchaser's preconceptions of how the goods or service should be supplied. This approach opens up competition, fostering lower prices and higher quality.

While each procurement is individual in nature, expressing an individual requirement, specifications should wherever possible adopt national or international standards or *de facto* standards, such as machine-readable cataloguing (MARC). In the longer term, the adoption of standards leads to reductions in the costs of both goods and services.

Cost is obviously an important element of any procurement. The specification should as far as possible address the whole-life costs of the requirement, addressing for instance reliability and maintenance costs. When buying or leasing equipment, costs of consumables, call-outs and maintenance should be taken into account, as well as the purchase or lease price.

The specification also provides the yardstick for evaluating any tenders received, so should be capable of being turned into measurable criteria. Obviously, this is easier for some procurements than for others. The discounts offered by booksellers on a basket of books can be compared easily one with another. However, concepts such as quality of service or the user-friendliness of a system are far more difficult to quantify. This should be borne in mind when drawing up any specification. How will one score suppliers against each other when evaluating their responses?

Perhaps the most complex specification that any library or consortium of libraries will produce is for a library management system. There has been some experimentation in drawing up a core specification for the procurement of library management systems. The Harmonize study (Fisher, Delbridge and Lambert, 2001) analysed 41 specifications from various libraries, discovering strong similarities in terms of functional requirements and some features specific to particular library sectors. In the USA, a project called OpenRFP publishes a website that aims to be 'an open marketplace, designed to increase the efficiency of the market for library software . . . [where] libraries can examine vendor software capabilities against their specific needs'. A UK core specification is also offered.

Finding the supplier
The tender

Often the marketplace is approached through a tender process. In the UK, this process is governed by the European Union's procurement directives. Issuing the tender document is the first step in a process leading to a contract between purchaser and suppliers. The involvement of procurement professionals from the start of the process is essential.

The tender document should give background information on the issuing organization and the procurement being undertaken, including how the tenders will be evaluated. A key element is the specification of requirements just discussed; this will in many cases be supplemented by a statement of the service levels required and any performance indicators.

The document also specifies the information required from the potential suppliers. This should include their audited accounts for the last three years, quality assurance accreditations, membership of professional organizations, qualifications and experience of key staff, evidence of commitment to staff development (Investors in People, policies, etc.), number of staff employed in key areas, and a list of major accounts. A selection from the last can be contacted for references on the performance of the supplier against key indicators.

A further important element required from potential suppliers is the price schedule. Several pricing models might be applied to library procurements:

- **Fixed price** – This is the most obvious model and the easiest to evaluate. It is used for one-off purchases or commissions, such as consultancy.
- **Discount from list price** – Hard-copy books and serials tend to be bought under this model, with intermediaries offering a discount from the cover price. While ostensibly simple, some care has to be taken when evaluating suppliers under this model to check that they are quoting the same price. Different approaches to exchange rates can lead to distortions.
- **Cost-plus** – In the past booksellers have tended to offer a single discount across the board. There is some risk for them in this model, since the discounts they receive from publishers or wholesalers vary: if customers order unexpectedly large numbers of titles offering low or no discount to the bookseller, they will lose money. Cost-plus eliminates this risk: the supplier charges the price paid for the items and adds a fixed charge for the work carried out. This model has attractions for both sides: the supplier has a guaranteed return; the purchaser knows that the best price is achieved. However, it can be difficult to audit and manage, and has generally not been offered by library suppliers.
- **Schedule of rates** – This model is often used in service contracts, for instance for maintenance of equipment, where charges for call-outs, time spent on-site, etc. are specified, perhaps varying between weekday and weekend.
- **Management fee** – Increasingly, LMS suppliers are offering a facilities management service, where they not only supply the system but also manage it. This model is generally used in such cases.
- **Fixed fee for each stage of completed work** – Buildings-related contracts often use this model, since it limits the financial risk to the purchaser of time

over-runs. It might also usefully be applied to LMS or other complex contracts where development is needed for the supplier to meet all parts of the specification.

Not all procurements are straightforward, of course, and contracts may include several of the above models for different elements of work. It is useful for the purchaser to be aware of the models in order to suggest to prospective suppliers which they might apply.

Evaluating the suppliers

Typically, a number of resources are used in the evaluation: published information and analyses (particularly financial), the returned tender documents, visits to suppliers' premises, customer references and meetings to clarify the information provided. Generally, there are four elements to be evaluated: the financial health of the supplier, the price quoted, quality and the ability of the suppliers to meet the specification:

1 Especially for contracts that are large, or last for a number of years, or are critical for carrying on the library's business (such as the library management system), one will want to evaluate the financial viability of the potential suppliers. The companies' audited accounts give information on turnover, profits and growth and performance trends. Organizations such as Dunn & Bradstreet provide overviews of the financial health of a company, compared with any industry standards. Databases such as FAME can also be used. The information secured should be evaluated by a friendly accountant or similarly qualified person.

Financial health is a pass/fail requirement. If there are justifiable doubts about the viability of a company, it should be rejected unless there are very good reasons to the contrary. No library will want to appoint a library management system supplier, for instance, that does not have the financial standing to invest in product development or may cease trading within the life of the contract.

It may also be inadvisable to award a large contract if it would form a significant proportion of a supplier's business. How will the supplier cope with the suddenly increased volume? It may be argued that the above tends to eliminate the small or new supplier, increasing the consolidation of the market. This is certainly a danger to be addressed in any tender, particularly in marketplaces that are shrinking. It is not in the purchaser's interest to decrease competition.

2 One will of course want to evaluate the price quoted, bearing in mind the different cost models discussed above, and the need to evaluate the cost over the whole life of the contract.

3 One will evaluate quality. This can be the most difficult area: quality is not easy to quantify, involving judgement rather than facts such as cost; moreover, one may well be in the position of judging the likely performance of a supplier with which one has had no dealings. There are some relatively concrete indicators, particularly accreditation under quality schemes such as ISO 9000 or Investors in People and membership of professional organizations. One may also take account of the qualifications and experience of key staff, and of staff development policies and programmes. Much information can also be gained from formal visits to suppliers' premises. These should be as structured as possible, with the team of evaluators having a checklist of quality measures under investigation. References from existing customers are also valuable. However, it is advisable to choose from a list of major clients, for instance all those spending over a certain amount with the supplier, rather than from a list of referees. The latter will be chosen by the supplier to give a favourable report; the former can be picked according the purchaser's interests. One should also ask the reference sites specific questions about performance and quality, such as supply times, rate of errors, customer care.

4 One may wish to evaluate the ability of the supplier to meet the specification. This applies particularly in procurements that are complex, such as a library management system, or seek to develop new services, such as shelf-ready books or supplier selection. Suppliers may not provide initially all of the functionality or services required; one will therefore need to judge how close they are to being able to meet the requirements.

Apart from the pass/fail requirement of financial health, the above elements of cost, quality and ability to meet the specification will differ in importance, depending on the situation of the purchaser and the type of procurement; one will therefore wish to recognize these differences by weighting the three elements accordingly. (A fully worked example of how one can apply weighting to complex decision-making is given at the end of Chapter 5.) In many cases, such as a contract for the supply of books, cost will be most important, and one might assign weightings of 40:30:30 respectively to the three elements. In other cases, for instance the procurement of a library management system, ability to meet the specification might be equally important; one might therefore apply weightings of 40:20:40.

Evaluating the suppliers: example

The following hypothetical example of a contract for shelf-ready books, for which three suppliers compete, illustrates the process. It is decided that the three elements will be weighted as follows: cost – 40; quality – 30; ability to meet the specification – 30.

Each supplier is asked to price the same basket of 100 books. Supplier A quotes £3200, Supplier B £3000 and Supplier C £2900. One easy way to express these prices as a score for each supplier is to award 100 to the lowest price and then express the lowest price as a percentage of the other prices. This process gives the following scores: Supplier A 91, Supplier B 97 and Supplier C 100.

Each of the areas comprising the other elements of quality and ability to meet the specification, of which examples are given in Table 4.1, is assigned an individual weighting. Each is scored out of 10 in the course of the evaluation process, and the total score is obtained by multiplying the raw score by the weighting.

Table 4.1 Evaluating suppliers 1

		Supplier A		Supplier B		Supplier C	
Quality	Weight	Score	Total	Score	Total	Score	Total
QA	2	8	16	7	14	5	10
IT system	2	7	14	6	12	6	12
Range supplied	1	8	8	7	7	7	7
Training	2	8	16	8	16	6	12
Customer care	3	8	24	7	21	5	15
Total	(10)		78		70		56
Meet Spec							
Edifact	2	8	16	8	16	8	16
Database	1.5	8	12	8	12	8	12
User friendly	1.5	6	9	8	12	8	12
Servicing	2	8	16	8	16	6	12
Shelf-ready	3	8	24	6	18	6	18
Total	(10)		77		74		70
Cost			91		97		100

Supplier C scores well on cost, but relatively poorly on quality, particularly quality assurance and customer care, which have quite high weightings. Applying the weightings assigned to cost, quality and ability to meet the specification, gives the results shown in Table 4.2.

Table 4.2 Evaluating suppliers 2

	Weight	Supplier A		Supplier B		Supplier C	
		Score	Total	Score	Total	Score	Total
Quality	30	78	2340	70	2100	56	1680
Meet spec	30	77	2310	74	2220	70	2100
Cost	40	91	3640	97	3880	100	4000
Total			**8290**		**8200**		**7780**

Even though cost has a greater weighting, Supplier C is still let down by underperformance on quality. If quality had been given an equal weighting, it would have scored even lower.

The approach outlined here demonstrates that it is possible to be rigorous even when evaluating and comparing the quality of service. The use of weighting adds a level of sophistication to the decision-making, enabling requirements to be reflected quite closely.

Awarding the contract

The deal is concluded. The obligations of the supplier and buyer, based on the specification, are written into a contract. The contract will normally be supplemented by service-level agreements and performance measures.

Measuring and monitoring suppliers' performance

The procurement cycle is far from over after the contract has been awarded. Contract management, the process of ensuring that specification, service-level agreements and performance measures are met over the period of the contract (which may be five years or more), is essential if suppliers are to be managed satisfactorily. This is generally achieved through quarterly or six-monthly contract review meetings with individual suppliers, who are expected to provide management information on the performance measures, drawn from the specification and detailed in the agreement. For a book contract these might include discounts achieved, time taken to supply books and to resolve queries, number of books supplied in error.

Conclusion

The above illustrates the procurement cycle. Fundamental to this cycle and its successful management is the specification of requirements: it is the basis both of selecting the best supplier(s) and of ensuring their performance throughout the life of the contract. It is crucial to produce a specification that reflects the purchaser's requirements accurately and fully, and in a form that can be quantified as far as possible. Writing the specification is not an easy process, but the time and effort expended at the start of the procurement cycle pay dividends throughout.

Managing suppliers and the marketplace

Turning from some of the techniques of procurement, a number of strategies have been adopted to manage suppliers and the market in which they operate. This section examines approaches to the procurement of hard-copy resources through traditional library purchasing consortia. It then turns to the procurement of electronic resources, looking at HE bodies that act as agents for the sector, how the traditional procurement model has been applied to electronic resources, and an attempt to develop a new model.

Library procurement consortia in the UK

Perhaps the most useful tool for carrying out procurements is the library consortium. Such aggregation of purchasing power brings many advantages. New services, for instance the truly shelf-ready – catalogued, classified and processed – book, have been negotiated through the strength of consortia. Quality of service is monitored closely and enhanced through continuing management of contracts based on tight specifications of service; pooled knowledge of suppliers' performance against these specifications lends force to this process. There are considerable savings in terms of the time needed by individual libraries to manage complex European Commission procurement procedures and the resulting contracts. Quite startling discounts on books have been obtained by UK consortia, for both public and academic libraries. As has already been discussed, these discounts are given from the intermediary's margin: the difference between the cost of a book to the intermediary and the published price. The intermediaries are in competition for market share, and will therefore cut prices and offer added-value services to gain such market share.

Consortia can be powerful entities, particularly when they take a holistic view uniting both print and electronic procurement: publishers produce and deal in both media; libraries integrate print and electronic forms in their service to users; they should integrate the procurement of them too. Consortia are the only library organizations that have a chance of affecting the marketplace; individual libraries certainly do not, given the conditions outlined in Chapter 2.

Collaboration between consortia

The situation in library procurement for HE in the UK is complex. There are seven regional purchasing consortia, covering together the whole of the UK, and with the majority of HE libraries in active membership. Some of these, such as the London Universities Purchasing Consortium, have grown from consortia responsible for procurement across the whole range of university activity. Others, such as North East and Yorkshire Academic Libraries, have grown from library collaboration, but have links to a wider university consortium. The value of procurement through their contracts is estimated at £70 million per annum. All the regional consortia, together with the Research Council libraries and the British Library, form Procurement for Libraries.

Procurement for Libraries aims to be a forum for the exchange of experience between consortia, to offer a unified voice to the HE sector, suppliers and other bodies, and to enhance procurement practice across the sector through staff development activities. It is also a forum where consortia can determine the appropriate level for any procurement, regional or national. The then Joint Procurement Policy and Strategy Group for HE, a body bringing together the general university purchasing consortia, established a protocol requiring a business case to be made evaluating the advantages and disadvantages of the national and the regional approach. Following this protocol, library consortia have generally adopted the regional approach for the supply of hard-copy resources: there are so few suppliers, particularly serials agents, that to award a national contract to only one or two might put the others out of business. The consortia are keen above all to promote competition in a healthy marketplace; acting nationally might severely damage competition and have harmful long-term effects.

The individual consortium

While size can be important for the individual consortium, in aggregating demand and providing libraries with a strong voice when negotiating with suppliers, it also brings problems. An HE consortium in the UK may have as many as 40 members, ranging from the small, very specialist performing arts institution, through the medium-sized research-oriented university, to the teaching-oriented university with large numbers of undergraduates.

Each of these types of institution will have a very different focus – extensive serials holdings or large quantities of textbooks for instance – and require very different specialist resources. The large geographically defined consortium will need robust mechanisms for consulting its members and ensuring that their diverse requirements are reflected in any procurements. Generally, this is achieved by plenary meetings, held once or twice a year, which decide strategy, and working groups, with representatives from the different types of library, which undertake the detailed work of the procurement cycle. These working groups have the advantage of enabling a number of people to be involved and build up expertise in the procurement process.

Given the diversity of the geographically defined consortia, and their some-times unwieldy numbers and spread, it may be argued that specialist consortia, representing only one type of library or a particular subject, could be more effective, and indeed obtain better prices for their members. However, it is possible to instigate joint specialist procurements by the regional consortia, through the mechanism of such groups as Procurement for Libraries discussed above. It is also possible to segment procurements by an individual large consortium, in order to develop specialist services, as the following discussion illustrates.

Traditional procurement of hard copy

A recent contract for books is given as an example of the operation of the traditional consortium contract for printed materials. This of course followed the standard procurement cycle, but had some interesting features.

The tender was undertaken at a time when:

- there was evidence of contraction in the marketplace and hence of a decreasing number of potential suppliers
- past contracts had demonstrated the value and quality of additional services such as the shelf-ready book

- new services such as slip and approval plans seemed to offer potential savings
- the market and business models for e-books were in a state of rapid growth and flux.

It was therefore decided to move away from the structure of previous tenders, which had split the business by place of publication – UK, Europe, North America, Rest of the World. The new tender was structured with the aims of:

- gaining maximum value and quality for the standard service, including shelf-ready books
- encouraging new services and new suppliers
- recognizing the use made by libraries of retailers, particularly those on campus.

Tenders were invited for one or more of the following lots: standard monograph supply, which had to offer a full and established shelf-ready service; standing orders; North American material; slip and approval plans; bookshops. This structure was held both to continue the standard supply of the bulk of materials for all libraries, to encourage innovative services and new suppliers, and for the first time specifically to bring retailers within the agreement. The outcome was the award of contracts to a number of suppliers for each lot, with some suppliers appointed for more than one lot, and with two suppliers being awarded contracts for the first time.

Electronic resources – applying the agent model

In the UK, two non-commercial organizations, the Joint Information Systems Committee and Eduserv/CHEST, act as agents for the HE sector in setting up agreements for electronic resources. They are not consortia, since they have no member institutions, but negotiate deals with content-providers and then offer them to the sector.

Firstly, there is the Joint Information Systems Committee (JISC), which was constituted to support 'further and higher education by providing strategic guidance, advice and opportunities to use Information and Communications Technology [ICT] to support teaching, learning, research and administration'. The JISC runs NESLi2, a national initiative for licensing e-journals on behalf of HE, which follows two earlier initiatives, the Pilot Site Licence Initiative (PSLI, 1995–7) and the original National Electronic Site Licence Initiative (NESLI,

1998–2001). The key features of NESLi2 are defined as:

- use of the Model NESLi2 Licence for Journals
- a clearly defined list of publishers to seek agreements with, based on feedback from the community
- an independent and experienced negotiation agent
- pre-defined criteria to assist the negotiation process
- flexible order channels and access routes.

NESLi2 currently offers agreements with a number of major publishers, including Blackwell, Elsevier, Springer and Wiley. It has more credibility than the original NESLI, with the role of the negotiating agent and the negotiating criteria clearly defined, and more developed channels of communication with the sector.

Another initiative is JISC Collections, which aims to provide a collection of online research tools, learning materials and digital archives for UK higher and further education. JISC Collections is open to approaches from any potential publisher, and does not confine its activities to the established commercial houses. It has a remit to enable access to innovative and niche resources, and will subsidize products in the early years of adoption.

Finally, there is Eduserv/CHEST, which 'negotiates for all forms of commercially available electronic resource (abstracts, full text, journals, software, courseware, etc.) for the education and research communities in the UK and Republic of Ireland, and . . . manages the resultant agreements'. Eduserv itself is a registered charity, wholly owned by the HE sector, and aims to make its agreements available as widely as possible. Products are sought only in response to demand from the sector.

It will be clear from the above that there may be some overlap in the resources provided by these agents. Thus, CHEST offers extensive collections of e-journals (such as Emerald Full Text, IEE Online Publications and PsycARTICLES) as well as databases (such as CrossFire Beilstein) and indexing and abstracting services. JISC Collections also offers abstracting services, full-text content and datasets, while NESLi2 offers full-text e-journal content.

There has also been a danger of the electronic deals offered cutting across the contracts with serials agents for hard-copy negotiated by the regional purchasing consortia. The latter may feature discounts related to volume of spending; members of such consortia have in the past lost discount because spending has been switched under the original NESLI to another serials agent or direct to the publisher. This fragmentation has now been recognized by the House of Commons Science and Technology Committee (2004, v1, p54), which, in response to evidence submitted by Procurement for Libraries, recommended that the JISC 'negotiate with libraries, regional purchasing consortia and other national bodies responsible for procurement to agree a common strategy'.

Electronic resources – applying the traditional procurement model

One example of the traditional procurement model, discussed above, applied to electronic resources is found in California. The California State University (CSU) libraries have operated as a consortium for more than 15 years, focusing on building system-wide access to electronic resources to support the core learning and distance curriculum (Healy, 1999). CSU runs a common curriculum across all its 21 campuses. There is therefore a natural overlap in journal provision. The Journal Access Core Collection (JACC) project team identified 1279 titles that were taken by at least 15 of the 21 libraries across the system. It then approached the market for the supply in electronic form of precisely these 1279 titles.

Key requirements for JACC included:

• a customized database of core titles selected by CSU, not tied to print subscriptions, nor to predetermined bundles of electronic journals packaged by publishers or aggregators
• JACC e-journal content equivalent to print in both content and currency
• open access for all authorized CSU users supported by open systems and compliance with Z39.50 for information access
• future access assured through vendor commitments to perpetual use and archiving solutions
• aggregation of content, content licences and access solutions.

The responses to the tender were revealing, in that no major publisher submitted a proposal. Four candidates progressed to the final evaluation, all intermediaries. The contract was awarded to EBSCO to run for 18 months from June 1999.

There are a number of interesting features of JACC. It sought to replicate precisely, in electronic form, a collection of print journals. It was customized, based on a very tightly defined set of requirements. It sought to evade one common problem: the packaging by publishers or intermediaries of the information made available to libraries in the form of bundles. JACC also took no account of the availability in electronic form of the titles required.

It is not clear what effect, if any, JACC has had on the price of journal titles; one assumes little effect, since the contract was placed with an intermediary, whose prices are dictated by the publisher. As in the traditional print model, there was in fact no attempt to deal directly with the publishers, the monopolists of information. The only competition was between intermediaries. However, CSU remained very much in control, defining requirements and terms, and retaining the libraries' position of authority, gained by virtue of selection of the titles.

Electronic resources – developing new models

Chapter 2 discusses at some length the development of new publishing models – open access and institutional repositories. Here, attention is turned to a new model for dealing with commercial publishers.

Pricing Electronic Access to Knowledge (PEAK) was a trial in electronic access, pricing and bundling by the University of Michigan and Elsevier Science. It provided access to approximately 1200 Elsevier Science journals for a period of 18 months to 12 campuses.

These institutions first had to buy a participation licence, which allowed searching of the database of articles. PEAK then offered three access models:

- **Traditional subscription** – Institutions and individual users could buy unlimited access to a set of articles that correspond to a print journal title.
- **Generalized subscription** – Institutional users could buy unlimited access to bundles comprising any 120 articles from the entire database of priced content. Articles were selected after the fact of subscription and could be accessed by all authorized users at the institution. Similar terms were available to individual users for their personal access.
- **Per article** – Individual users could buy limited access to a specific article for a fixed price.

PEAK is a most interesting model for almost the whole of the information chain: to the publisher it offers some degree of stability of income; to the library and its patrons it offers flexibility of collection and selection; it also offers the possibility of devolving purchasing decisions to the end-user.

As far as the publisher is concerned, the two subscription models replicate, or are at least similar to, current pre-payment practice. Publishers therefore have the prospect of some guarantee of stability of income in what could be a transition to a completely different payment structure. Moreover, the purchase from the publisher of individual articles for personal use has the potential to divert an income stream from intermediaries, in the form of document delivery services, to the originating publisher.

As far as the library is concerned, spending is, as now, limited by budget rather than driven by usage. However, at the same time, there is a great degree of flexibility in the selection of material, which should allow libraries to provide, within budgets, what their users require, rather than what is offered in publishers' bundles. The traditional subscription model is similar in effect to JACC, facilitating the purchase of core 'cover-to-cover' titles. The generalized subscription model breaks the tyranny of the title, allowing libraries to build the eclectic collections their users require. Publishers would retain their position of authority, through the editorial process, but the importance of branding inherent in the serial title would diminish.

The purchasing decisions in the generalized subscription and per article models can be devolved as the institution wishes: to the subject librarian, to faculty representatives, to individual members of academic staff or even the student body. This devolution helps to overcome the economic discontinuity of the traditional subscription model noted in Chapter 2: the user in general does not pay for the information used; payment is made from an institutional budget delegated to the librarian. With the PEAK model, individual users are much closer to controlling the spending of budgets in accord with their needs; this should result in better value for money from library spending.

The PEAK experiment telescopes the information chain, cutting much of the mediation between end-user and publisher. This is to be applauded as a general principle, even though it does call into question the future of intermediaries – libraries, subscription agents or document delivery services. If the model were to become general, with several publishers participating, there would be a major requirement for systems to manage the search and retrieval function and the payment (presumably by e-commerce) function; this might fall naturally to the subscription agents. While libraries lose some of their power of branding and authority, since they may no longer be the sole aggregators in the institution, there would remain a major procurement role for them in defining requirements and systems, and in procuring the greatest value for money for their users.

A generally applied PEAK model, with the major publishers participating, might also have interesting implications for the position of publishers as monopolists. With purchasing decisions made at the level of the individual article, there may be more intense competition between publishers on content, price and terms of use. On the other hand, with document delivery providers increasingly cut out of the chain, the monopoly position of publishers as suppliers of information would be enhanced.

Conclusions

As far as procurement in traditional library areas – hard copy and library management systems – goes, methods and mechanisms are well established. The general purchasing consortia have brought significant cost savings and have enabled the development of major new services, such as the shelf-ready book and approval plans. The standard procurement cycle, centring on a tender process to a tight specification and subsequent contract management, has proved its effectiveness. Libraries should, therefore, actively support the purchasing consortia.

The procurement of electronic resources is, as one might expect, not so well developed. There has been very little integration or co-ordination with the procurement of hard copy. This is unfortunate, since, particularly with journals, it is very difficult to separate the two: electronic deals often have hard-copy elements, and the same intermediaries may be involved. Except in the case of JACC, there is little evidence of the standard procurement cycle being followed. Instead, in the UK a number of bodies act as agents, reaching agreements that they think will please the HE library market. Although NESLi2 shows improved practice, PSLI and the original NESLI allowed publishers to establish business models not necessarily advantageous to the purchaser.

As discussed in Chapter 2, traditional hard-copy publishing in peer-reviewed journals is deeply entrenched because of institutional and personal interests in the scholarly community. Alternative publishing initiatives can, however, be held up as models, even if there is little chance that in themselves they will become rivals to traditional publishing. As Guédon (2001, 16) remarks, pitting SPARC (the Scholarly Publishing and Academic Resources Coalition) against the big publishers is like pitting David against Goliath; one might add that Goliath has the added advantage of having chosen a stone-free field of battle. Libraries should continue to support initiatives such as SPARC.

Finally, librarians should involve their users more. Many of the current and historical problems are exacerbated by divorcing the user from payment for information. This is not to suggest that the user should be made to pay, rather that the economic consequences of their demands should be made clear to them.

Models such as PEAK enable this. Librarians might also involve them more in the procurement cycle. How many consortia or individual libraries consult the end-user about the specification or include them in contract management?

5
Outsourcing and externalization

Introduction

In recent years, there has been increasing interest in the UK in the concept of outsourcing public-sector services. This has been manifested in public libraries, firstly by compulsory competitive tendering and, secondly, by the encouragement of public–private sector partnerships, through such schemes as the Private Finance Initiative (PFI) and Public Private Partnerships. The latter approaches open up new possibilities for funding public service provision and the operation of the resulting asset by the private sector. Interest in future outsourcing in libraries also derives from continuing budget restrictions, both revenue and capital, and, in the local government sector particularly, a purchaser/provider culture.

This chapter examines both outsourcing, which is defined as 'the contracting of activities to an outside individual or organization (which may be another publicly funded body) in place of the use of in-house staff' (Boss, 1999), and externalization, 'which is the process of providing all aspects of the current service through a trust or company established specifically for the purpose' (Ball et al., 2002). Some of the activities traditionally outsourced are discussed in Chapter 3; the focus here is on the benefits and process of large-scale outsourcing of whole activities.

Lessons are drawn from the public library sector, which, because of the culture of compulsory competitive tendering and Best Value, has more experience of outsourcing. This sector also offers many interesting examples of services being outsourced to other public-sector bodies, not to commercial companies; this trend may be of particular application for university libraries in catering for distance learners and others based away from the university campus.

The chapter also offers a decision matrix, recommended for judging the potential within an organization for outsourcing.

Studies of outsourcing by libraries

There have been two large-scale studies of outsourcing by libraries. The first was undertaken by KPMG and Capital Planning Information Ltd (CPI) for the Department of National Heritage on contracting out in public libraries (KPMG and CPI, 1995). This study concluded, among other things, that:

- the application of the contracting process was feasible
- contracting out should be seen in the context of its ability to help the service achieve its aims
- the prospect of significant reduction in cost was limited
- there was no natural marketplace for the provision of the range of services; there was, however, a market for elements of the service
- the low level of activity in acquisitions-related outsourcing suggested benefits were doubtful.

The second study (Ball et al., 2002), undertaken in 2000–1, had a wider scope, paying attention to HE, public and special libraries and, to a more limited extent, museums and archives. This study concluded that some of the KPMG/CPI conclusions were still valid: there was limited potential for cost-savings; the concerns about diminution of service and an erosion of the culture of co-operation remained. However, there had been significant movement in important areas: there was much greater experience of contracting, which was becoming second nature in many sectors; there was widespread de facto outsourcing of some activities (e.g. library acquisitions); the marketplace for large-scale and whole-service outsourcing was starting to appear. One can, therefore, conclude that there has been a significant trend towards outsourcing and externalization in the years between 1995 and 2002; there is no reason to suppose that this trend will not continue.

The goals of outsourcing

Throughout the literature two main reasons for outsourcing are given: to reduce costs and to focus on core activities. Tom Peters, for instance, is quoted as saying you should do what you do best and outsource the rest (Bordeianu and Benaud, 1997).

Marcum (1998) distinguishes between tactical manifestations of outsourcing, to cut costs, and the strategic use of outsourcing, to focus on core competences. As part of a strategy, outsourcing usually involves restructuring and re-engineering to gain competitive advantage. He also sees it as a component of other broader trends in business life: efforts to de-bureaucratize, and general privatization and downsizing.

There is no guarantee that outsourcing will reduce costs. Outsourcing is most likely to be cost-effective if the workload is cyclical, i.e. it fluctuates during the year so the organization is periodically over- or understaffed. A vendor may be able to realize economies of scale, or utilize technology or other equipment to which the organization does not have access (e.g. expensive imaging equipment). One major problem is that most libraries do not know their costs, so it is difficult to determine accurately how much money is saved (Boss, 1999). Reducing a temporary backlog and acquiring expertise not available within the regular staff are other frequently cited reasons for outsourcing (Boss, 1999).

In his book on outsourcing government service, O'Looney (1998) gives the goals as: to reduce, make more efficient and reform government services. Efficiencies are achieved through restoring competition, tapping economies of scale and discovering the most efficient production techniques. Workers in the private sector in areas frequently outsourced by governments tend to be paid less and receive fewer benefits than comparable government workers. There may, therefore, be a moral dimension to outsourcing strategy and decisions.

One fear often cited is loss of control. An interesting example of such loss occurred during the fuel protests in the UK in summer 2000. Most of the oil companies have outsourced the transport of fuel from refineries or depots to petrol stations. The new contractors are often independent hauliers, one-person businesses, who may well be former employees made redundant by the oil companies. In consequence, the oil companies were unable to order drivers to cross picket lines as they may well have done had they remained employees (Hutton, 2000).

The process of outsourcing

The process of outsourcing has three commonly identified phases: planning, implementing and managing. There are obvious echoes of the previous chapter's discussion of the procurement cycle.

Planning

This phase requires by far the greatest concentration of time and effort and includes the often painstaking process of gathering data.

Fischli (quoted by Marcum, 1998) notes that outsourcing should be a component of a larger process re-engineering project rather than a tactic for reducing costs. If a library's strategy is to switch staff from back-room to front of house and academic liaison, outsourcing of book selection, cataloguing and processing are obvious candidates.

There are five major steps in the planning phase:

1 The first step involves assessing the feasibility of the outsourcing project. What is the potential provider market? Clearly, if there are no potential service providers, then outsourcing is not possible. Care must be taken to consider the service in the light of policy criteria. It is also important to consider if contracting out will affect existing co-operative arrangements and networks (Missingham, n.d.).

2 The next major step involves examining and costing internal workflows and operations. There are two methods of determining such in-house costs:

- The *time-task analysis* method involves all staff keeping a diary about the activity. The cost is then the value of hours (salary plus benefits) and all indirect costs (supplies and equipment, including administrative overheads and cost of space).
- The *total output measure* method involves determining the total budget for an activity: all salaries, benefits and indirect costs. This method works well if an entire activity, such as cataloguing and processing books, is to be outsourced (Boss, 1999).

3 Once all current costs are known, the next step involves the development of a detailed specification for the outsourced service. This will include such information as:

- the desired contractor's knowledge of, and compatibility with, existing systems
- what facilities a potential contractor must provide
- how work will be monitored and quality ensured
- whether the contractor works in-house or from their own premises.

Further, the pricing model, for instance a flat management fee or a cost per unit, should also be considered (Grimwood-Jones, 1994).

4 The next step is the preparation and advertisement of a tender based on the detailed specification of, for instance, cataloguing and classification requirements, selection criteria. Staff involvement in the planning stage is important to minimize resistance; they can also provide the expertise required to develop a suitable specification.

5 Finally, once a suitable vendor has been chosen, it remains to negotiate the contract.

Implementation

This is the most disruptive phase. It involves rearranging workflows, introducing new routines, developing new policies and learning new systems. Work must be integrated with that of the vendor. This phase is usually intense, but should not last long (Bordeianu and Benaud, 1997).

Managing

The real issue is not outsourcing, but the responsible management of outsourcing (Boss, 1999). Once the outsourcing contract is established, there remains the continuing process of monitoring quality performance and troubleshooting. For outsourcing to be effective there is a need to refrain from micro-managing the project: quality checking has to be selective and there has to be a high level of trust between the two parties (Bordeianu and Benaud, 1997).

The library will need to retain experienced staff to oversee the outsourced operations. For example, in the case of outsourcing collection development, an experienced librarian must ensure that the books sent match the library's profile and must identify any gaps in the collection (Bordeianu and Benaud, 1997). Typically, the library will see a trend towards employing fewer paraprofessional staff, but increasing management responsibilities.

Current practice in outsourcing and externalization in libraries

The broad picture, outside the special library sector, is one of piecemeal outsourcing of technical activities, e.g. acquisitions. The future offers the prospect of consolidation into the outsourcing of whole activities, if not services.

Public libraries

Part-service outsourcing

Materials supply and processing have long been an area of outsourcing; more recently, libraries have outsourced the cataloguing and classification of the bulk of their materials to suppliers so that the items arrive fully shelf-ready. As shown in Chapter 3, suppliers now also offer to select books for libraries against set criteria. This broadening of processes outsourced could lead eventually to the whole of stock management (including acquisition) being outsourced.

Information and communications technology (ICT) is also a long-standing area for outsourcing. Most public libraries have bought in turnkey library management systems, rather than designing a system in-house. One exception is Dorset County, which has recently contracted a software house to develop its own in-house system to replace an existing in-house system of several years' standing. The advantages of outsourcing lie in the areas of cost and technical skills. Most recently, public libraries have offered internet access and electronic resources through the installation of the People's Network. Facilities management may be outsourced. This happens in a number of ways: to the system supplier, to an ICT contractor, or to another authority (e.g. following local government reorganization).

For many years, especially following the contracting-out legislation of the late 1980s, local authorities have contracted out support functions such as cleaning and maintenance. The library service has had these functions outsourced as part of an authority-wide process. There is also evidence of the outsourcing of library-specific functions, particularly the recovery of library books from defaulters. This too may follow authority-wide practice.

A range of special services has been considered for outsourcing. Examples include:

- the provision of mobile services by one authority for another (especially following local government reorganization)
- the outsourcing of the supply and operation of transport, usually as part of an authority-wide process
- micro-franchising, i.e. the operation and management of a branch library by a lesser authority (e.g. a parish council taking responsibility under a formal agreement for the operation of a small library).

More recent proposals relate to:

- the delivery of the housebound service being undertaken as part of a contract for the delivery of home meals
- the outsourcing of call centres, including a library telephone enquiry service
- the outsourcing of business information services.

Following local government reorganization a number of part-service outsourcing arrangements were entered into, some temporary, but some continuing, where one authority provides a range of services to another. The best example of this is Essex, which provides a range of services, including provision of ordering and supply service (itself outsourced by Essex) and an ICT system for Thurrock and Southend Boroughs. Another example is the operation by Dorset County of a schools library service in Bournemouth and Poole Boroughs as well as in the County, rather than three separate services being established.

This trend is evident in the statistical database (CIPFA Statistical Information Service, 2004). In 2002–3 total income for public libraries in the UK from the provision of library services to other authorities was about £2.4 million. The bulk of this went to the English counties, and seems to be a result of local government reorganization: unitary authorities, split out of larger services, contracted for work to be done by the former parent authority.

Whole-service outsourcing

The only example of a whole service outsourced is Hounslow, which, in 1998, established a trust to provide its leisure services, including the library service, which was set up as one of the companies within the trust. The service is now provided under contract to the library authority by the trust. The main benefits are claimed to be a greater freedom of action to respond quickly to new developments and changes, greater budgeting certainty over the period of the contract (ten years with a mid-point break and funding linked to the retail price index) and a board, representing a cross-section of the community, which can fight for the service.

There is at least one example of the management of a library service being outsourced to a commercial supplier (Edmonds, 2003). Following an Audit Commission report that Haringey Libraries were 'poor' with 'no prospect of improvement', the Borough appointed Instant Library Ltd to manage the service. The Borough has experienced a huge improvement in service, owing partly to the fresh management approach, but also to additional investment (£200,000 per year on the book-fund) and the introduction of the People's Network. It is perhaps also significant that the library service's reporting line was transferred to the Chief Executive's Department.

At the time of writing outsourcing of a complete service to a commercial supplier, such as by Riverside Public Libraries in the USA (Dubberley, 1998), has not happened in the UK.

Private Finance Initiatives

Private Finance Initiatives (PFIs) are intended to introduce private capital into the public sector, essentially to fund major capital projects, which the public sector finds difficult to finance. It is a form of deferred capital financing providing the asset immediately, but with long-term costs being incurred as the private sector partner recoups costs and makes profit on the asset before it is handed over at the end of the term of the agreement. The most obvious example is the provision of the new central library for Bournemouth Borough, together with the delivery of a new ICT system, subsuming the library management system, for the whole service.

PFI involves enormous inputs of senior local authority staff time, as well as the employment of expensive specialists, but, if the alternative is no new capital developments, the advantage to the service and users may be easy to identify.

There may also be a lack of flexibility: for instance, choice of the main building contractor by Bournemouth Borough determined the ICT contractor involved, which in turn determined the choice of supplier for the library management system. This is not to imply that an inappropriate system was installed: the vendor in the successful consortium has a large share of the public library market. Rather, the freedom of choice of key IT contractors and systems by the library service was lost, together with the potential for joint arrangements with neighbouring libraries and other innovative approaches.

Academic libraries

The contracting out culture that we see in local government does not pervade universities, nor have they been subject to the large-scale reorganization that has led to many outsourcing arrangements in local government. In general, universities have been resistant to outsourcing the operation of their ICT systems, for instance, claiming that the ICT systems are integral to their teaching and business processes. One exception is the University of Durham, which has outsourced its management information systems.

Private Finance Initiatives

PFIs are also comparatively rare in HE: universities operate under a very different financial regime from local authorities, and perhaps find it easier to raise capital than local authorities. Except for student accommodation, there are probably fewer opportunities to produce income streams from university buildings. It is, for instance, unlikely that university libraries will be an integral part of town-centre shopping developments.

A guide issued by HEFCE (2004b) notes that PFI offers one of the main benefits of outsourcing, the import of the specialist expertise of a commercial partner. It is, however, held to be an inappropriate route for projects involving a capital investment of less than £20 million, partly because of the management overhead already discussed. Local government has been able to bundle projects together to achieve this threshold more readily than HE.

PFI is seen as a possible route for projects that:

- provide a service as well as a capital asset, giving the private sector scope to manage the balance between capital and operating costs
- offer scope for risk sharing: the commercial partner would, for instance, be more likely than a university to find alternative use for residential accommodation
- offer better value for money, providing a service more cheaply or to higher quality.

While many projects have the potential for income from third parties, this is not seen to be essential.

Generally, PFI is applied to non-core functions. Other sectors show successful projects involving the provision of car parks, offices, residential accommodation, catering services, sports and conference facilities, and combined heat and power services. This is another example of the product-to-service shift: the accent is on buying access to and use of facilities, rather than acquiring an asset outright.

Many of the PFI projects within HE have involved the provision of student residences, which obviously bring an income stream and offer scope for the commercial provider to take some share of the risk. Other projects, for instance for telecommunications and heat and power, are less common. Projects providing teaching or research facilities, including libraries, are least common.

Other activities

As we have seen, some academic libraries, partly owing to the influence of the purchasing consortia, obtain their stock in shelf-ready form, but there is a greater reluctance in the academic sector to outsource the cataloguing and processing operation than in the public library sector. The particular needs of the institution are often claimed to require a specialist approach to the cataloguing and classification of materials. Classification schemes are often idiosyncratic, with frequent modifications, extensions and mixing of editions. Cataloguing and classification are still seen as core professional functions, and guarded as such.

Varying degrees of activity are reported between higher and FE libraries, which tend unsurprisingly to reflect institutional attitudes and levels of collaboration. Some FE institutions have contracts with the local university (e.g. Middlesex) for the delivery of a library service. There are indications that this type of arrangement will become more common. To the author's knowledge one university and its four associated colleges have a common library management system, which is run from and maintained by the university; the colleges pay a fee. Another university has a well developed network of associate colleges, and within that an inner core of colleges calling itself the Higher Education and Training Partnership. The university now provides one college with library facilities seamlessly with its local campus library. Each year the college is invoiced for an agreed sum to cover stock and staff. Mergers of HE and FE institutions have generally meant that the university has taken responsibility for the college library.

Externalization

Externalization of HE library services to companies, which are generally wholly owned by the institution, is fairly common. The Society of College, National and University Libraries (SCONUL) is aware of at least twelve HE libraries operating in this way. We may therefore assume that as many as 10% of university libraries fall into this category. These companies are generally associated with new building projects, and are seen as tax-efficient. Library staff are generally seconded to the company; the HE institution leases premises to the company and charges for overheads and services; in return, the library company invoices the HE institution for library services delivered. This practice is analogous in some ways to trust formation in the local authority sector, such as Hounslow's Community Initiative Partnership. Once externalized, there is no evidence that these HE library companies seek to trade except with their HE institution. They remain, however, potential vehicles for providing commercial services to other libraries.

Views of suppliers

Libraries are only one half of the equation. For outsourcing to work well, there must also be a market of suppliers willing and able to provide the range of services required. Lack of such suppliers was identified as an inhibitor by the KPMG and CPI study (1995). More recent studies have shown that the marketplace has expanded.

Suppliers of both whole-service and part-service outsourcing were surveyed by Ball et al. (2002, 55–6). Common themes are:

- **Standardization** – If libraries are able to move away from complex requirements, for instance in ordering and processing books, consortia and co-operatives especially could gain substantial savings by outsourcing to the private sector. In some cases (e.g. classification), software might be developed to cater for local variations.
- **Scale** – Full facilities management of stock against specified criteria is seen to be both feasible and in prospect. With stable contracts over a period of, say, five years, suppliers could provide financial and other benefits through application of their specialist skills and economies of scale. Length of contract is important to suppliers – from the point of view of set-up costs, continuity and staffing stability.
- **New ways of working** – Companies jointly owned by a supplier and a library authority have been proposed. The political climate of public–private partnerships favours this option.
- **Regionalization** – This is seen as providing an opportunity for externalization and joint arrangements between libraries.
- **Technology** – Teleworking is mentioned as a possibility by a major supplier of bibliographic services, to enable its employees to work at library sites rather than at the company's offices. Regional and joint arrangements obviously support this distributed way of working, creating nodes of greater activity.
- **Whole-service versus partial outsourcing** – Whole-service outsourcing is generally confined to the commercial sector and to the relatively small library (i.e. not public or academic) in the public sector. Instant Library Ltd offers wide-ranging expertise from over 150 specialist staff. This results not only in

whole-service outsourcing but also in consultancy and other work (e.g. library design) for larger services where Instant Library has developed particular expertise.

- **Facilities management** – There is seen to be increasing scope for IT-related companies to win facilities management contracts. Often they will work as part of a consortium, not alone. Benefits to the outsourcer are transfer of risk to the contractor; economies of scale (e.g. servers, systems management); cheaper services than in-house IT departments.
- **Partnership** – It is stressed that outsourcing does not bring only cost savings, flexibility and efficiencies. It also adds value by making available a high level of professional expertise. Suppliers are stressing more and more that the outsourcing relationship, whether whole- or part-service, is a partnership that can deliver the highest value by operating at the strategic level in the customer organization. Obviously, there is a level of self-interest here: all suppliers seek to make themselves as indispensable as possible. There is, however, a valid point, familiar to all involved in procurement: good suppliers are expert in their own business; this expertise is best exploited by the customer when the supplier is given the freedom to offer solutions and development, rather than being strait-jacketed into client-specified legacy routines and practices.

Perceived problems

In higher education, learning resources, particularly libraries, are closely integrated with teaching. While the Quality Assessment Agency (QAA) now operates with a 'lighter touch' as regards subject provision, professional bodies such as the Law Society are still exacting, and there remain the QAA's quinquennial institutional audits. Provision is monitored closely by the external quality assurance bodies. Demonstrating the integration of the provision of appropriate resources into academic process and strategy is fundamental to satisfying these bodies, and may affect a university's position in the unloved league tables. There may well be resistance to what may be seen as a surrender of control to a supplier through the outsourcing, for instance, of book selection.

In the FE sector, by contrast, outsourcing to an HE partner may be seen and portrayed as an enhancement to both level and quality of service. Quality, and equality, of access to resources for HE students in the FE environment will continue to be closely scrutinized by the quality agencies. (See Chapter 6 for a full discussion.) Outsourcing library provision in FE colleges to an HE partner may well bring not only economies of scale but also comfort as to quality of provision.

Concern has also been voiced that, as the outsourcing market matures, service to individual institutions may diminish. The feared dynamic is that while a library is a single and leading customer for a service, great attention will be paid to the customization and delivery of the service to that library; however, when there are many customers of equal value, the customization may disappear and a lowest-common-denominator or cloned service become the norm. This fear is not really justified: as with all procurement of goods and services, specification of requirements and management of contracts delivering those requirements are fundamental to the quality of service procured. As outlined in Chapter 4, the importance of applying procurement expertise to tenders, specifications and contract management will grow.

Volatility in the commercial sector may also be of concern. There has been considerable turbulence in the book and serials supply markets: Dawson's serials business being sold to RoweCom, then to divine, then to EBSCO, and Blackwell's serials division and Swets merging are just two examples. Instant Library Ltd has been taken over by the Tribal Group. Librarians are well aware of the problems that can arise as suppliers of a single discrete service (e.g. books or serials) change ownership. There is a danger that such turbulence will be magnified if whole services are outsourced to the private sector. This danger is exacerbated by the fact that the marketplace for outsourced services is relatively immature.

Tools and techniques

Chapter 4 discusses in some detail the tendering and contract management process. Clearly, this same process, based on a tight specification, also underlies successful outsourcing. One danger often cited is that of turning to outsourcing as a means of resolving a poorly understood problem. This fault may lie at the root of many outsourcing failures. How can one write a proper specification of the process or service to be outsourced if one does not fully understand it? As Chapter 4 stresses, a well written specification is fundamental to any contractual process, and this is especially true of outsourcing.

Decision matrix

Before entering the tendering process, one must first decide whether a service or process is actually a suitable candidate for outsourcing. A useful technique is the weighted decision matrix.

Building on an example developed by Marcum (1998), Ball et al. (2002)

identified nine cultural, economic and functional factors that merit consideration when assessing the suitability of a service or process for outsourcing. These factors are:

Cultural factors

- **Peripheral to service identity** – If a service or product is seen to define or be core to the library's relationship with its users, particular consideration should be given to the advisability of having it provided by a third party. Examples of core services might be creation and maintenance of the content of a library's website, and stock selection.
- **Complies with corporate strategy(ies)** – In the UK local government sector, Best Value implies that all services must be tested against any outsourced equivalent. The commercial sector will generally have a strategy of seeking low-cost flexible solutions. Increasingly the academic sector will follow the other two. However, the outsourced solution may conflict with other corporate strategies. For example, a university may have a policy of supporting local businesses and employment; outsourcing a service where there are no local providers runs counter to this policy.
- **Corporate policy** – Secondary services, such as cleaning and security, may be outsourced as a matter of corporate policy.

Economic factors

- **High revenue cost** – One main reason for outsourcing is that specialist suppliers should be able to offer economies of scale or innovative delivery of service. Given a properly constructed contract, such economies will be shared with the customer. The higher the revenue cost, therefore, the greater the potential financial benefit of outsourcing.
- **High capital cost** – Public sector organizations in particular often face constraints on capital investment. Outsourcing to the private sector is one means of easing such constraints.
- **Market/suppliers exist** – It seems obvious that, if there are no prospective suppliers, there is little possibility of outsourcing a service. One may further question the wisdom of outsourcing a service to a monopoly or near-monopoly supplier. The economic rationale for outsourcing a service is to benefit from the effects of competition in depressing prices and increasing efficiency and service. Where there is no competition, prices rise at the whim

of the monopolist, and there is no motivation for efficiency. Having outsourced a service, it may be very difficult to bring it back in-house. Organizations may also wish to consider creating suppliers through regional or other collaboration.

Functional factors

- **Difficult-to-deliver service** – There are many reasons why a service may be difficult to deliver. There may be sudden unpredictable peaks of activity or demand. Maintaining in-house staffing levels to cope with the peaks may be impossible; the specialist contractor will have much higher capacity. Opening service points outside core hours may be impractical or very expensive using directly employed staff, but achievable using agencies. There may be no in-house expertise for specialist work, such as design; there may be a lack of specialist knowledge, for instance relating to health and safety.
- **Poor or declining performance** – 'If it ain't broke don't fix it' is a useful precept. If, on the other hand, there is dissatisfaction with a service an innovative approach by an external supplier working to tight performance measures may bring both cost-savings and increased user satisfaction.
- **Easy-to-specify service** – One view often advanced is that routine tasks are easiest to specify and also bring benefits in terms of cost-savings and enhanced performance when outsourced. The procurement profession would hold that it is possible to construct a specification for the vast majority of services or products. Difficulties tend to arise from a lack of clarity on the part of those writing the specification. While this contention is fundamentally true, the lack of clarity is itself an impediment to outsourcing: if one cannot describe one's requirements for the market place, suppliers will not be in a position to meet them. This factor may in fact indicate an internal organizational immaturity rather than a difficulty in specifying and procuring the service. However, the immaturity itself would be an impediment to success in outsourcing.

It will be apparent from the above that some factors contradict others. For instance, a high-revenue-cost activity might imply both a high level of in-house expertise and a non-peripheral service. Obviously individual libraries will balance the different factors as they see fit. The factors may be applied in the following ways.

Simple matrix

The first is a straightforward matrix. The factors are simply listed; the more ticks in the right-hand column(s), the more likely is the service to be a candidate for outsourcing. See Table 5.1. It is worth noting that this is not a prescription: a profile of ticks to the right suggests a service as a suitable candidate for an outsourcing exercise, not that it should be outsourced. That remains a decision for management.

Table 5.1   A simple decision matrix for outsourcing

Factor	No			Yes
Cultural				
Peripheral to service identity				
Complies with corporate strategy(ies)				
Corporate policy				
Economic				
High revenue cost				
High capital cost				
Market/suppliers exist				
Functional				
Difficult-to-deliver service				
Poor or declining performance				
Easy-to-specify service				

For instance, analysis of a café run in-house might produce the profile shown in Table 5.2. The library would then form its view as to the importance of the factors in the left-hand half of the grid. Despite the low cost implications in this hypothetical example, the potential of the practicality of an outsourcing solution (the suppliers exist; the service is easy to specify) and of turning around a service perceived as poor may make this a prime candidate.

Libraries will, of course, expand or otherwise modify the matrix. When considering whole-service outsourcing, for instance, they might expand the corporate strategies element. A university might assess compliance of outsourcing its library service with its strategies for information, learning and teaching, regional involvement, and research, as well as with the strategies of the institution as a whole and of individual faculties. It may well be that integration of the library service and its staff with the academic process and with quality assurance is central to the

Table 5.2   A simple decision matrix applied to outsourcing a library café

Factor	No			Yes
Cultural				
Peripheral to service identity			✓	
Complies with corporate strategy(ies)			✓	
Corporate policy		✓		
Economic				
High revenue cost	✓			
High capital cost	✓			
Market/suppliers exist				✓
Functional				
Difficult-to-deliver service				✓
Poor or declining performance				✓
Easy-to-specify service				✓

Table 5.3   A simple decision matrix applied to whole-service outsourcing of a university library

Factor	No			Yes
Cultural				
Peripheral to service identity		✓		
Complies with information strategy				✓
Complies with learning and teaching strategy	✓			
Complies with research strategy	✓			
Corporate policy				✓
Economic				
High revenue cost				✓
High capital cost		✓		
Market/suppliers exist		✓		
Functional				
Difficult-to-deliver service				✓
Poor or declining performance			✓	
Easy-to-specify service		✓		

learning and teaching and research strategies, while pursuit or consideration of outsourcing is central to the overall institutional and information strategies. This could yield the profile shown in Table 5.3. The university would then form its view. The left-hand half of the grid shows a slight preponderance; a contra-indication may be the importance to the institution of its overall or policy and the information strategy. Again, these are matters for judgement, political as well as economic. The purpose of the matrix is to inform that judgement, not to substitute it.

Weighted matrix

Libraries may wish to refine the matrix by assigning weightings to factors. In the last example, for instance, it was suggested that the university might assign a higher weighting to its overall strategy and its information strategy. Weighting may be achieved by grouping factors into bands and assigning numerical values to the degrees of compliance. To take a simple example, an institution facing severe financial restrictions might apply the weighted model shown in Table 5.4.

Table 5.4   A weighted decision matrix for outsourcing

Weight	Factor	No			Yes
		1	2	3	4
3	High capital cost				
3	Market/suppliers exist				
3	High recurrent cost				
2	Complies with corporate strategy(ies)				
2	Poor or declining performance				
2	Easy-to-specify service				
1	Peripheral to service identity				
1	Corporate policy				
1	Difficult-to-deliver service				
				Total	

The score is arrived at by multiplying the value of the degree of compliance by the weighting. Thus, the cash-strapped library might assess the provision of an in-house bindery as shown in Table 5.5.

Table 5.5   A weighted decision matrix applied to outsourcing a university library bindery

Weight	Factor	No			Yes
		1	2	3	4
3	High capital cost			9	
3	Market/suppliers exist				12
3	High recurrent cost				12
2	Complies with corporate strategy(ies)	2			
2	Poor or declining performance			6	
2	Easy-to-specify service		4		
1	Peripheral to service identity			3	
1	Corporate policy	1			
1	Difficult-to-deliver service		2		
				Total	**51**

Table 5.6 shows how the same library might assess another candidate for outsourcing, book selection. The profiles are quite similar if one takes account only of distribution across the two halves of the matrix. Both have four entries in the left-hand columns and five in the right-hand columns; if all factors are given a weighting of one, the bindery scores 24 and supplier selection 22. However, the weighted score shows the bindery as the more appropriate candidate to meet the library's requirements, with a score of 51 against 43 for supplier selection. This application of the matrix is therefore of use in comparing a range of services as candidates for outsourcing against corporately defined criteria.

The weighted matrix is a useful tool for assessing services and processes as candidates for outsourcing. It is not a substitute for a professionally conducted procurement process. Once the decision, informed by use of the matrix, to approach the market is made, normal procurement practice must be adopted. It is at this stage that factors such as cost and quality of service will be assessed. The level of risk of the potential contract can also first be assessed at this stage. Only then will the status of the contractors and the resilience of the marketplace become clear.

Table 5.6 A weighted decision matrix applied to outsourcing book selection for a university library

Weight	Factor	No			Yes
		1	2	3	4
3	High capital cost	3			
3	Market/suppliers exist		6		
3	High recurrent cost				12
2	Complies with corporate strategy(ies)	2			
2	Poor or declining performance			6	
2	Easy-to-specify service			6	
1	Peripheral to service identity	1			
1	Corporate policy			3	
1	Difficult-to-deliver service				4
				Total	**43**

Conclusions

Outsourcing is a significant feature of the public and commercial library sectors in particular. This is both because it is recognized, when properly managed and applied, as a valuable tool for decreasing costs and improving quality of service, and because of the climate of Best Value in public libraries. The culture of tendering and contract management, a prerequisite for successful outsourcing, is becoming more embedded. The increasing incidence of grant funding will reinforce this trend.

There are inhibitors for the process of outsourcing, particularly the granularity of the marketplace and concerns about the effects of arm's-length delivery of service. While PFIs are seen as a means of introducing capital investment to public library services, they are not a significant element of HE culture.

As many as 10% of universities have externalized their library services to companies. Others are providing library services to FECs. There is, however, no evidence of the externalized companies actively seeking business outside their parent institutions; other imperatives (e.g. inter-institutional collaboration) have driven the provision of service to FE.

The standard procurement cycle is fundamental if the full benefits are to be gained from outsourcing. This is based on a full, tight specification of the service to be provided, implemented through close and continuing contract management. Other tools, such as the weighted decision matrix, can be developed as an aid to the process of managing outsourcing.

6
HE–FE relationships
Jane Ryland and David Ball

Introduction

Partnerships between higher education institutions (HEIs) and further education colleges (FECs) in the UK exist under a variety of guises; many are longstanding. They range from the bilateral relationship, between one HEI and one FEC, to consortia of large numbers of institutions, with a wide range of programmes covering a whole region or more. Some were formed during the rapid expansion of HE in the late 1980s and early 1990s; others are more recent, following widening participation initiatives.

Academic matters

In England, the responsibility for HE in FECs now generally rests with HEFCE, which offers FECs three funding routes:

- direct funding from HEFCE to an individual FEC
- indirect funding through an HEI (generally, but misleadingly, known as 'franchising')
- indirect funding through a consortium of FECs, generally with at least one HEI.

(This chapter follows HEFCE terminology of direct and indirect funding, concentrating on the indirectly funded relationship.) There is general encouragement for FECs to work in partnership with an HEI, particularly in order to develop appropriate quality assurance arrangements. According to HEFCE (2002) statistics for 2000/01, 36,000 HE students were taught in an

FEC; 60 HEIs and 262 FECs were partners in indirect funding agreements. The numbers of HE students taught in FECs rose by 11% to over 40,000 the following year (HEFCE, 2004c, 4). As outlined in Chapter 1, this number will rise further because of the foundation degrees (FDs) now coming into being, which are taught almost exclusively in FECs, and because FECs are seen as a means of delivering wider participation in HE.

A review of indirect funding arrangements in England by the National Institute of Adult and Continuing Education (NIACE) et al. demonstrates the extent of such arrangements, which involve more than half of all HEIs and two-thirds of FECs (2003, 51). One of the main drivers for entering such arrangements as far as HEIs are concerned is regionality, or the need to respond to relatively local demand for HE provision. For FECs, the arrangements are seen as the only practical way of obtaining significant HE student numbers. The review notes a degree of dissatisfaction on the part of FECs, particularly as regards perceived inequality in the relationship, and the level of funding retained by the HEIs.

While the Quality Assurance Agency (QAA) recognizes that the best relationships between HEIs and FECs are characterized by 'equity, integrity and honesty', it also points out that the HEI awarding qualifications bears the responsibility for the quality of those awards. This responsibility suggests 'a conscious formality' in managing the collaborative relationship, which may appear to run counter to the principle of equality (2004, 2). It also insists on the necessity of legally binding contracts, setting out the rights and obligations of the parties, and stresses that the awarding HEI is ultimately responsible for the quality of learning opportunities offered under any collaborative agreement.

Library matters

Partnerships between HEI and FEC libraries generally arise from the arrangements for collaborative teaching provision, and are naturally influenced by the nature and tenor of the institutional partnerships. Of particular concern to the HEI library, as embodiment of the awarding institution, is the quality of learning opportunities offered in the FEC. The study by Goodall and Brophy (1997), carried out in 1994, gives a good picture of the challenges and highlights good practice. The main practical problems are attributed to difficulties with funding allocations – HE textbooks are very expensive. Journals are also difficult to afford, and are not well used because they are not promoted by teaching staff in the FECs. The FE-focused study environment and the difficulty of developing an appropriate information skills programme with limited staff resources are also cited.

Goodall and Brophy note the cultural differences between higher and further education: FEC librarians generally were not involved by college management in deliberations about the introduction and support of HE courses. Both relationships with academic staff and management, and communication structures were felt to be lacking. As far as HE librarians were concerned, services and support appeared 'to be offered half-heartedly', with the FECs and students kept at arm's length. Little if any change in the services offered by HE libraries was apparent as a response to increasing access for HE students remote from the HEI.

The recent survey (2003) by the Chartered Institute of Library and Information Professionals (CILIP) of learning resource provision in FECs offers perhaps the fullest picture yet achieved of the FE sector as a whole. There are, depressingly, many echoes of the problems documented by Goodall and Brophy ten years earlier. The survey confirms that about two-thirds of FECs have HE provision. A few have large numbers of students – two report more than 3000 – but the majority report less than 500. There is no correlation between the number of HE students and library provision, or between the number, level and range of programme areas and the size of the library budget. While nearly 90% of libraries offer access to electronic resources within the library, only 42% replicate such access remotely; 90% of libraries spend at least 75% of their budget on printed materials. The survey reflects the low status of FEC library staff, compared with colleagues in HEIs: only 25% of college librarians describe themselves as heads of department or senior managers; the rest describe themselves as middle managers or administrative officers. While membership of college committees is quite widespread, the survey finds 'a very low level of actual involvement or engagement'. There is no correlation between status or engagement with committees and HE provision. The survey concludes: 'Many colleges provide library services with minimal staffing levels, using staff with inappropriate qualifications or staff without access to relevant CPD [continuing professional development] activities. College senior managers may feel that they are providing a full, effective and efficient library when, in fact, they are simply making available an open space that lends books and has access to the internet.'

HE libraries are responsible for the quality of service delivered at one remove by FEC libraries to HE students; the above indicates some of the additional difficulties facing HE libraries in forging effective partnerships to deliver high-quality services. It is in the interests of both HEIs and FECs to deliver HE in the

FE environment; however, they have very different perceptions of the partnership and the way it operates. Each HEI typically has partnerships with a number of FECs, some with very small HE numbers compared with their overall number of students. Library provision is overwhelmingly in hard copy; budgets seem to bear little relation to the number and level of programmes offered. Library staff generally lack the status and engagement with the academic process to give them a strong voice with FEC management.

Solutions

In suggesting how one may address some of these problems, this chapter discusses:

- establishing effective relationships
- strategic management of the partnership
- delivering effective service provision
- ensuring high-quality services and resources
- establishing external relationships
- the future.

Much of the discussion is particularly relevant to supporting distance learning, whether delivered through an FEC or not.

Establishing the relationship

There are difficulties inherent in establishing effective relationships between libraries to support HE in FEC students. The relationship has not been sought by libraries but has been imposed by the nature of the franchising agreement. From a practical point of view, it can be difficult to fit appropriate HE services into the FEC environment: FEC libraries often lack space for quiet study, IT facilities may be inadequate and opening hours may not meet the needs of HE students.

Delivery of HE in FEC courses is complex and it is not always clear where responsibilities lie. There is a danger that the HEI will be perceived as taking on a Big Brother role; this can lead to resentment and lack of co-operation on the part of the FEC libraries. Poor communication resulting from geographical remoteness, lack of time and lack of co-ordination can aggravate the situation and lead to further misunderstandings. FEC library staff do not generally have sufficient knowledge of HE resources or the needs of HE students to provide effective support – a fact that is often not appreciated by HE library staff.

Communication

Many of these difficulties can be overcome by good communication and a sensitive approach to the relationship by the HEI library. Clarification of roles is essential and needs to be undertaken in co-operation with the FEC libraries to avoid setting unrealistic targets. Service-level agreements can be an effective approach, provided that they are drawn up sensitively to take into account the considerations of the FEC libraries. Arnold (2002, 51) provides an example of the service-level agreement between De Montfort University Library Service and its partner institutions. Where an HEI has several partner FEC libraries, all with different capabilities and methods of delivery, there is a danger that one service-level agreement would be either so specific that not all the partners can meet the terms or so general as to be effectively useless. Multiple agreements might raise issues about equity of provision.

An alternative solution to service-level agreements is to draw up an information sheet or web page for the students and use this to guide service delivery. Again, this should be a collaborative effort. Even where a service-level agreement exists, such a document (a service-level statement) needs to be drawn up for the students to ensure that they are aware of their entitlement and of the range of library services available.

Good communication between the HEI and FEC libraries and a flexible attitude can help to resolve any misunderstandings that may arise from the nature of the partnership. It is therefore essential when establishing a relationship to develop formal channels of communication. These can include regular meetings of library managers, an e-mail discussion group and an individual at the HEI who can act as a central conduit for information. Communication needs to reach staff working at an operational level as well as library managers.

Training and support

Support mechanisms should be identified and set in place when establishing a relationship. A training programme needs to be initiated that will help FEC library staff to develop skills in exploiting HE resources, to enhance their knowledge of the needs of HE students, and to develop an awareness of appropriate HE materials. Training should be carried out ideally by an HE in FE specialist librarian who has extensive experience of HE resources and has strong communication links with the HEI's subject librarians. Alternatively, training could be conducted by the subject librarians but should still be delivered at the FEC library. This enables the subject librarians to gain a greater understanding of the FEC environment and to intercept potential access problems.

Once initial training has been delivered, a plan needs to be drawn up to ensure that training is ongoing. Continued support is vital to keep the FEC library staff up to date with changing resources, to refresh their skills and to support new staff.

Strategic management

Management

Once a relationship has been established, it requires ongoing management at strategic level if it is to be effective. The overall management of the relationships should take place at a senior level with library managers from both the HEI and the FEC co-operating to develop services. Where appropriate, key staff in the wider environment, such as academics and fund-holders, should also be involved in the decision-making process. Library services need to be represented at a strategic level in the wider institutional context and senior library staff should be members of relevant committees in both the HEI and the FEC. Close involvement in collaborative provision not only benefits the students but also can help to enhance the reputation of the HEI library (Arnold, 2002, 51).

Many HEIs have now established units with responsibility for certain types of special provision, including HE in FECs. These units are important sources of information that is useful for libraries, such as changes to courses, strategic matters and funding issues. Strong communication links with such units are vital to the successful management of services.

Co-ordination of services is essential, especially where one HEI has several FEC partners. These individual relationships should be viewed as a single network and, where possible, decisions should be made that are appropriate across the network. This enables the HEI to ensure an equitable level of service to all its students. It also permits libraries within the network to share experiences, knowledge and information. However, there are substantial differences between the individual FEC libraries and decisions must be made to reflect these differences. FEC libraries should know what they need to achieve but must be allowed the flexibility to implement services in a way that best suits their service. Standards are essential but one size does not necessarily fit all.

When a network consists of a number of libraries, it is easy to lose sight of the overall picture. The co-ordination of services therefore needs to be allocated to an individual librarian with strategic responsibilities. Ideally, this role would be combined with the role of the HE in FE specialist because this person has a first-hand view of the service and is able to relate to the wider issues of HE in FECs. Regular contact with FEC library staff opens up two-way communication so that the HEI library is also aware of any relevant changes that take place within an FEC.

The role of the HE in FE specialist was successfully piloted, with substantial HEFCE funding, by the Dorset, South Somerset and South Wiltshire (DSW) Higher Education Partnership. A full account of this developing role is given by Ryland (2004).

Planning

In the early years of HE in FEC provision, libraries in many ways tried to replicate HE services within the FEC environment. It was felt that these students should receive the same experience as a student studying at the HEI. This proved not only impractical but also undesirable. In the mid-1990s, Goodall (1996, 6) drew attention to the fact that the HE in FEC experience is unique and that FEC libraries should not seek to duplicate HE library services but to provide services that are appropriate to the very specific needs of these students.

Some FECs have succeeded in using HE provision as a bargaining tool for introducing services that mirror those offered in HEI libraries, but which can be appropriately implemented in the FE environment. For example, some have introduced an enquiry or information desk service that is separate from the general circulation desk. This allows staff to respond to subject-specific questions in greater depth than would be possible at a busy general desk. Similarly, some FEC libraries have introduced a subject librarian structure. This enables individual staff to develop specialized knowledge in the resources of a particular subject area and so offer better support and training for the students. It also supports the integration of library staff with course teams, as they are able to attend course team meetings and be more involved in course activities.

Such initiatives are useful for staff development as they enable staff to specialize in a subject area. Staff generally find working with HE students rewarding: they tend to be enthusiastic and want to learn. Improved staff development and enhanced morale are important in the FEC environment where staff recruitment and retention are problematic, often due to low salaries. While the overall number of staff is often small, the low proportion of professional staff is of particular concern. Training by HEI staff can help to alleviate some of these issues but FEC librarians need to continue to lobby for better staffing levels.

When planning services, libraries need to take into account the unique nature of the courses and the students. While the academic needs of non-traditional students have been well documented, there is less understanding of these students' information needs, especially those studying for foundation degrees. The needs of indirectly funded students were well documented from both the HEI and FEC perspectives when so-called franchising arrangements first started. However, this is not true of foundation degrees, which are new and very different from existing courses, and so have different resource needs. From a library perspective, the precise level and type of resources required is not yet fully apparent.

Library staff therefore need to work closely with both FEC and HEI teaching staff to ensure appropriate resources. They may even find a discrepancy between the views of FEC and HEI teaching staff, as FEC staff tend to work in a more textbook-oriented environment, whereas HEI staff tend to use more complex resources. HEFCE guidelines (2003a, 21) strongly support the use of journal articles and more advanced resources, and library services should provide training opportunities for FEC staff to ensure that they are confident in the use of HE resources.

Libraries also need to be involved at a strategic level in the planning process for new courses. If they are not involved at an early stage, it may be impossible to provide adequate resources to meet the course plan. It is the responsibility of the FEC library staff to participate in this process but support should be provided by the HEI. HEI library staff can advise on appropriate resources and services and can share their experiences of the process. They may also have influence with the academic staff at the HEI if they feel that there may be a problem. FEC and HEI library staff need to work together to ensure that adequate start-up funds and subsequent ongoing funds are allocated.

Funding

Funding structures vary across institutions depending on how much of the available funding is directed to the FECs and how much (if any) is directed to the HEI library. This can have a significant impact on the decision-making process. For example, in HEIs where the large majority of the funds are allocated to the FECs, expenditure is more likely to be concentrated on building up the resources in the FEC library than to support an inter-campus loan system.

Regardless of the method of funding, HEI and FEC library staff need to work together to ensure adequate budgets. As has been noted already, there is generally no correlation between FEC library budgets and the level and range of provision. Despite the fact that for indirectly funded students FECs receive a separate and identifiable funding stream from the HEI, FEC libraries generally do not receive a separately identified budget for HE students. Budget cuts generally are applied across the board, which in effect means that HE funds are subsidizing FE provision. FEC librarians are placed in an impossible position: HE student numbers may very well be small, compared with overall numbers, and the resources, particularly journals, expensive; yet they are under pressure to maintain spending for HE students to the detriment of the majority.

FEC managers responsible for allocating funds therefore need to be aware of the need for a protected, separately identifiable HE budget that will continue to meet the needs of HE students. FEC library managers need to ensure that they have sufficient influence in the organizational structure to implement changes to support HE students and to ensure funding to provide adequate facilities, services and levels of staffing. Clearly, HE librarians should also apply whatever pressure they can in support of their FE colleagues.

This is an area where guidelines or standards for provision might be useful, particularly since there is no statistical database for FEC libraries similar to the SCONUL statistics for HE libraries. HE librarians are able to point to expenditure per full-time equivalent student, averaged across all HEIs or at peer institutions; their FEC colleagues do not have this ammunition. CILIP is currently addressing this by producing a set of guidelines drawn from the experiences of practitioners nationwide. Brief guidance is also offered by HEFCE (2003a) although this report concentrates primarily on course delivery.

Service provision

Collaboration between HEI and FEC libraries is needed to ensure effective delivery of the three main areas of service provision – resources, training and services. The focus of the provision needs to be on the FEC library as this is where the students are studying, but a high level of support is also needed from the HE library.

Resources

Print resources are generally provided by the FEC library. In addition, some HEIs give the students full membership of the HEI library, some offer free postal returns and some an inter-campus loans service to supplement the resources available. FEC libraries are often small, reflecting poor budgets, especially where there is no separate HE budget, and lower student numbers overall. There is also less opportunity for the multiple use of stock as only a very small proportion of students studying in an FEC are studying at HE level, so stock purchased for other students will be inappropriate. However, as a result of long-term HE funding, many FEC libraries are starting to build up their collections and, while students will always complain about lack of books, the problem is less critical for some than it has been in the past. FEC library collections remain small compared with HEI collections; this accentuates the need for students to make good use of online resources.

Online resources are generally provided by the HEI library through its website. While in theory ideally suited to supporting remote provision, practical problems do arise. Database providers, whether intermediaries or publishers, may be reluctant to extend access to a third party: any institution gaining 'free' access is regarded as a lost potential sale. The HE intermediaries such as JISC and Eduserv/CHEST are of course aware of the needs of HE in FEC students, and are tending now to include indirectly funded students in their standard licences. Otherwise, institutions have to negotiate extensions to licences to include such students. (See Chapter 3 for a fuller discussion.)

The status of the teaching staff of an FEC is also problematic: they generally have no direct relationship with the HEI, and are not its registered students. They will therefore not be covered by the licences generally in use. This gives rise to the significant anomaly that, while students have access to electronic resources, the staff teaching them do not. It has been demonstrated in surveys (Foy, Spencer and Ball, 2002) that this lack of access by FEC staff affects take-up of electronic resources by HE students in FECs. One neat solution adopted by some universities is to give FEC staff teaching their courses a contract of (unpaid) employment, enabling access to all university resources and hence also creating a greater feeling of identity with the university.

Usage statistics of online resources by HE in FEC students tend to be very low. This can be attributed to a number of factors. In addition to the lack of promotion of online resources by teaching staff, these students do not fit the traditional HE student profile and may not have the same confidence or skill in using computers as the student who has recently left school. The FE environment is still print- and textbook-oriented and students may simply be unaware of the range of resources available to them online. There may also be practical barriers to accessing resources. Sometimes there are problems caused by the way the network has been set up in the FEC. Computers may not be sufficiently up to date to ensure smooth and relatively fast searching, and numbers may be inadequate. Password administration is rather complex and some students may have two Athens passwords – one for the FEC and one for the HEI.

Some of these issues are disappearing as more people own their own computers and systems are generally improving. The real key to promoting use of online resources, however, is training.

Training staff

The importance of training FEC library staff to increase knowledge and awareness of HE resources has already been discussed. It is then their responsibility to deliver training to their students and staff. Again, it should be a collaborative action with HEI library staff offering advice in the planning stages and even helping to deliver sessions in some circumstances, for example when training teaching staff or when the FEC librarian is new or is tackling a new subject area. It is often up to the individuals concerned to decide whether this is helpful and the HEI staff should be flexible in their approach and sensitive to the needs of the FEC staff.

The importance of training teaching staff in the use of online resources cannot be underestimated. It helps them to form a better understanding of the resources available when planning course work and it provides them with a valuable resource to inform their teaching. It is also the most effective way of encouraging the students to use the resources. If the teaching staff act as advocates and advise the students to use specific online resources, then they are far more likely to use those resources. If they are prepared to go one step further and embed some form of information skills training into the curriculum or link the library session to an assignment, then the students have little choice but to explore these resources.

The difficulty for many FEC library staff is to persuade teaching staff to attend training sessions. This can be attributed to a number of factors. These include lack of time due to heavy FEC timetables. Training sessions therefore need to be promoted so that they stand out as something different that will attract attention, for instance as part of a staff training day. It may be possible to bring in an external speaker from the HEI or the JISC Regional Support Centre and turn the session into a mini-seminar.

In many FECs the librarian's role is undervalued and teaching staff do not perceive that they can learn anything from them that will support their teaching. Many library staff are paid on an administrative pay scale and are considered to be administrators rather than information specialists. FEC library managers are constantly lobbying for at least their professional staff to be employed at demonstrator or academic level but it has proved extremely difficult to get the unique skills of library staff recognized by FEC decision makers.

Probably the most significant reason why teaching staff do not attend library sessions is lack of awareness of the importance of the resources. Some may not even be aware that they exist, unlike their colleagues in HEIs for whom online resources are an integral part of their working environment. Persuading staff to give up valuable time to learn about something that they are not aware of is a very difficult task. The best approach is to raise awareness of the online resources using as many different methods as possible. These can include promotion through e-mail bulletins, intranet or VLE pages, champions or staff with influence (especially those with appraisal or line-management responsibilities), course meetings, events such as validations, inspections and reviews, and new staff inductions.

FEC teaching staff are now being required to study towards FE teaching qualifications. It is therefore important for library staff to get to know the leader of these programmes within their college and to persuade them to introduce a library information skills session into the programme. Similarly, it is often possible to create interest in online resources through externally funded projects. Many teaching staff like to be involved in such projects as they are seen as high-profile activities and possible useful additions to their CVs.

Informal communication can be a very powerful way to promote HE resources. Encouraging teaching staff to become more involved in library activities in general helps to spread the message about the resources and services that the library can offer. None of this is easy and it requires patience, persistence and imagination on the part of the library staff.

Training students

Library staff need to consider similar issues when planning a training programme for students. HE students today tend to focus heavily on grades. This is due to a number of factors such as pressures of time, especially if students are working to support their studies, financial pressure to do well and the target-oriented culture of the secondary education system. While HE in FEC students may generally be more interested in developing a wider view of their subject than traditional students, they tend to have greater external pressures. As a result, it is difficult to encourage students to attend sessions that are not directly linked to an assignment or grade.

If teaching staff can be persuaded to embed information skills into the curriculum or link the sessions to an assignment, library staff can at least be assured of reasonable attendance. However, in the current climate, this is often not possible and library staff need to find ways to target the students directly by tapping in to existing communication networks. For example, when students first log in to their computer profile, there may be space for bulletins or there may be existing e-mail groups that reach a wide group of students. It is important to talk to students by attending meetings where they or their representatives will be present or by tapping in to tutorial sessions. Collaboration with other services, such as learning support and careers, is useful as they are often in a position to refer students to the library.

In the worst case, where teaching staff are unwilling to give up teaching time for library sessions, it may be possible to approach the students to arrange a session in their own time. This can succeed where students are studying for vocational HE qualifications in subject areas with a strong information focus, such as marketing.

One difficulty inherent in delivering training to HE in FEC student groups is the range of abilities encountered within each individual group. These students tend to come from a wide range of backgrounds and so have different life and educational experiences, and different levels of competence. Library staff therefore need to be prepared to be flexible and to tailor a session to the needs of the group. It is important to stress to those who appear to be struggling that they can come back for individual help. Similarly, those who wish to explore beyond the materials covered in the session should be encouraged to return for further guidance. Worksheets enable students to work at their own pace but the librarian still needs to ensure that they are not devoting too much time with one individual at the expense of others.

Virtual learning environments (VLEs) are starting to play a key role in FECs and many library staff are becoming involved in their development. VLEs can be useful tools for supporting library training for HE in FEC students. They can be used simply as a central location for access to learning resources, such as websites, JISC resources, databases and library catalogues. Provided that this location is prominently placed, students are likely to explore the links as part of their regular navigation of the VLE.

Some libraries are going one step further and developing virtual information skills packages to be included on their VLE. These packages need to be developed in close collaboration with IT staff, who can provide the design and the technology, while library staff provide the content. It is also useful to involve teaching staff in the planning and testing stages. For HE in FEC students, the package needs to be highly interactive and intuitive. The content needs to be fairly basic and should assume no prior knowledge. In this way, the package can be accessible for a wide range of students regardless of their geographic location, ICT competence or previous educational background.

VLE packages are generally not used to replace actual training sessions but rather to support them. They are useful for students who may have missed their scheduled training or as a refresher to reinforce the training. They are useful for the many HE in FEC students who live or work remotely from the college and therefore are not able to see the library staff in person when they have queries. Some students simply learn better using online packages. An added advantage of working with VLEs is that it enables library staff to work more closely with academic staff and so enhance awareness of the library's contribution to the learning process.

Services

One of the reasons that many students choose to study in their local FEC is that they are likely to receive better individual support than in what is perceived as the more impersonal HEI environment. This emphasis on individual support should be reflected in the library provision of enquiry services. Those libraries that have a separate enquiry desk or specialized subject librarians must be vigilant in their promotion of these services to their HE students. Those that do not need to look for other ways of ensuring that individual support is available and that students are aware of it. Training sessions are useful for promoting enquiry services, as the student is more likely to seek an individual that they recognize from these sessions.

Enquiry services offered by the FEC should be supported by library staff at the HEI. FEC library staff should be able to contact the subject librarians at the HEI to help with difficult queries or those that require resources beyond those available at the FEC library. Students should also be able to contact the subject librarians themselves and have access to any virtual enquiry services available to HEI students.

FEC library staff need to be aware that the nature of the individual support they provide should not inhibit independent learning. HEFCE guidelines (2003a, 21) indicate that self-directed learning is an essential element of HE study. FEC library staff need to be aware that they should show students how to find the information themselves and not find it for them; this can be difficult for some FEC library staff who feel that they are then being unhelpful. Library staff training therefore needs to stress that their role is different when dealing with HE students in that they should see themselves as guiding and informing the students to enable them to become successful self-directed learners.

Quality assurance

QAA guidelines (2004) clearly state that quality assurance for HE in FE courses is the responsibility of the awarding HEI. However, monitoring and ensuring quality needs to be a collaborative activity between the HEI and the FE libraries. As the number of students studying HE in FE increases, the pressure to demonstrate that high-quality services are being delivered also increases. This has taken on added significance since the QAA announced that inspections specifically targeting collaborative provision will take place starting in 2005/6.

HEI and FEC libraries need to work together to ensure the best possible results in QAA and other inspections. FEC librarians can draw on the expertise of the HEI subject librarians in preparing for inspections and both parties should maintain documentation on a continuing basis as evidence of good practice. Librarians need to work together to ensure their early involvement in the planning process and to present a united view of the library service during the inspection events.

HEIs need to set in place good-quality systems that can be used across their network of FEC partners. These systems need to take into account the differences between individual colleges but also ensure an appropriate standard of service. This can be problematic where individual colleges can differ significantly from each other, but can be achieved by focusing on the core elements of provision.

The checklist approach

One approach developed by Bournemouth University is a quinquennial evaluation of the library services provided by each of its partner FECs. The approach (see the Appendix for the full document) is developed and adapted from the LINC Health Panel Accreditation Working Group checklist for health libraries supporting HE. It also draws on SCONUL's *Aide-Mémoire for Assessors when Evaluating Library and Computing Services* (2003) and CILIP's (then The Library Association) *Library and Learning Resources Provision for Franchised and other Collaborative Courses* (1999).

The checklist is divided into three areas:

- **Library strategy, planning and liaison** – This covers questions such as whether the library's mission statement reflects that of the FEC and the university; the position of the library in the FEC organization; whether the library has a current quality assurance programme; whether there is input into course planning.
- **Resources** – This section asks whether there is a separate HE budget; whether staffing is adequate and if there is a staff appraisal system; whether the accommodation and equipment are appropriate.
- **Learning materials** – This section addresses the availability and relevance of learning resources in all formats; the arrangements for loans and interlibrary loans; the level of electronic resources provided; and whether there is an appropriate information skills programme.

For each question there is a statement reflecting an expectation about the service and suggested forms of evidence. On liaison, for instance, the statement might be: 'there is input from the library to course planning, development and delivery, including attendance at validation events'. The evidence might include: membership and minutes of committees, correspondence, staff sampling. There are boxes to detail the evidence, for the assessee (the college librarian) and the assessor (usually the university librarian) to comment, and for agreed actions. The checklist is given to the college librarian in advance, and the comments by the assessor and any agreed actions completed during an evaluation visit.

The completed checklists provide a base-line in assuring the quality of provision in partner FECs. They document and evaluate the service provided in each FEC, noting particular strengths and any areas for improvement. These areas are monitored each year for progress, and a fresh evaluation is carried out every fifth year (to coincide with institutional audit). The documents are useful in a formal respect: they have been submitted to external validation and peer-review bodies as evidence of the quality of provision; they are also submitted to internal quality and development committees. They are also used less formally, for instance by partner FEC librarians as evidence of their requirements for supporting HE provision.

The checklists have been used for about seven years by Bournemouth University. The evidence from them is of significant improvements in all aspects of provision in the partner FECs. These improvements are obviously due to the industry of library staff and to a high level of collaboration. The contribution of the checklists themselves to prompting, focusing and recording improvement should not be underestimated.

Other quality assurance mechanisms

The comparative lack of status of and engagement in deliberative committees by FEC librarians has already been noted. Involvement in important quality assurance events, such as external peer reviews, validations and the evaluation discussed above may help to rectify this. It is also incumbent on HE librarians to increase the engagement of their FE colleagues. This may be achieved in part through their own positions on HEI deliberative committees. It may also be valuable to form a consultative committee to focus on collaborative library provision. Such a committee might involve senior library staff from the HEI and FECs, HE managers from the FECs and senior HEI staff with responsibility for quality of provision in partner institutions. It would also report into the deliberative structures of both HEI and FECs.

Turning to other quality assurance mechanisms, obtaining feedback from students and staff is clearly essential for monitoring quality. A single annual survey can be devised to obtain feedback from students across the partnership. The core questions should remain the same from year to year to monitor improvements, but questions can be added or removed to take into account changes in provision. A similar survey should be devised for teaching staff to provide feedback on library services and on attitudes. Results from the surveys should be compiled in a report and actions highlighted and the FEC library staff should be invited to comment on issues specific to their library. The final report can be used to show improvements and also as a tool for attracting improved funding.

Database statistics can be used to track patterns of use of online resources and can help to indicate the level of impact of training programmes. Similarly, most

FECs maintain internal statistical data that can be especially useful if HE students are monitored separately.

Statistics and surveys can present an incomplete picture of the views of students and staff about library services, as they tend to provide quantitative rather than qualitative data. Some qualitative feedback can be obtained by asking a member of the teaching staff to give up 10–15 minutes at the beginning of a tutorial for a member of the library staff to talk to the students about library provision.

External partnerships

The critical partnership for HE in FEC provision is that between the HEI and its partner FECs. However, other significant relationships can develop in the HE in FEC context. The network that links the HEI to its partner FECs allows a natural partnership to develop between the individual FECs. FEC library staff often feel isolated, especially if located in rural areas. Contacts with the library staff of other FECs enable them to establish a support network where they can share ideas, resources and even staff. Such a network can be particularly effective in supporting staff development opportunities where, for example, staff numbers are too low in individual colleges to support mentoring networks or even to release staff for development opportunities.

HEIs can also benefit from establishing links with other information providers in the area. Public libraries, special libraries, museums and archives are all useful sources of material and support that may help to enhance the learning experience; they are also often much closer to where the students live than the HEI. Students may go to the public library for a quieter or more convenient place to study. They may also visit local information providers for specialist information to support their studies. Formalizing links with these providers can help to manage student expectations regarding what is available, exploit the full range of materials and expertise available locally, and encourage students to make greater use of publicly available resources. Such arrangements also benefit other learners distant from the HE campus.

In order to formalize these links, a group of representatives from all parties could be established to discuss the feasibility of potential initiatives. Library staff from the educational institutions and students need to be aware of the resources and services that are available elsewhere. Similarly, staff at other institutions need to be aware of the type of query the students may have and to know when and how to refer them to their college library. Information sheets, informal training sessions, visits and mutual links on websites can all be employed to deliver this information.

Conclusions

The relationship between HEI and FEC libraries is not necessarily an easy one, primarily because of the differences in culture between the institutions, the unique nature of the courses, the modes of delivery and the student profile. It is also a relationship that has been imposed rather than sought out and needs to be handled with flexibility and sensitivity. However, if the relationship is managed well, it can bring benefits to the libraries and ensure a high-quality service to the students.

The application of relatively small amounts of infrastructure funding to the FEC libraries can have a major impact. This has been the experience of the DSW HE Partnership, which, through funding from HEFCE, has managed to improve the base-line library management system technology and access to electronic resources in the partner libraries. Working in partnership to apply the funding, together with the concrete results, has also led to a greater commonality of purpose between the FEC and HEI libraries.

The recent introduction of foundation degrees has reinforced the message that HE in FEC is here to stay. This is supported by the number of HEIs winning additional student numbers for HE in FEC provision and increased scrutiny of collaborative provision. For many HEIs, these students make up a significant proportion of their total numbers and these numbers seem set to increase. In addition, the range of courses is increasing as foundation degree provision expands.

It is therefore time for libraries to bring HE in FEC provision into the mainstream. The only effective way to achieve this is for HEI and FEC libraries to work in close collaboration at the strategic level and in relation to service provision and quality assurance. While relationships with external organizations can be established along the way, it is the partnership between the HEI and FEC libraries that is the key to successful support.

Important elements in developing and sustaining a productive partnership are:

- an understanding of the fundamental relationship between, and hence the responsibilities of, the institutions
- openness and sensitivity at all levels to the characteristics of the different sectors

- a formal but developmental periodic evaluation of service provision
- the development of appropriate deliberative structures that involve all relevant staff
- the identification of one senior member of staff of the HEI library as having primary responsibility for liaison and communication with and development of partner FEC libraries.

7
HE–NHS relationships
Jill Beard and David Ball

Introduction

The importance of the National Health Service (NHS), one of the world's largest learning organizations, for HE is discussed in Chapter 1. Relationships between HEIs and the NHS are very complex; this is hardly surprising, given that one in 20 of those in employment in the UK works in the NHS, and that the organization is committed to continuing professional development for its whole workforce. The size of the NHS and its commitment to learning make it the most complex and most commonly encountered manifestation of the practice of work-based learning in the UK.

This chapter takes the NHS, and particularly nursing education, as its focus, because of their importance to HE and because most of the lessons can be applied to the provision of any work-based or distance learning. It begins by examining the determining features of the relationships between HE and the NHS and library responses to them. Following the structure of Chapter 6, it then discusses how libraries can work successfully in partnership with colleagues in the NHS.

Background

Partnerships between HE and the NHS, like those between HE and FE, exist in a variety of guises; many of them are longstanding. The relationships are driven by NHS bodies contracting with the HEIs to provide education and training for future and existing employees. They frequently cover cognate discipline groups, such as nursing and midwifery, and are governed by the recruitment needs of bodies covering large geographic areas, with perhaps more than one HEI delivering the education. At the other extreme there are small post-registration or post-experience contracts between one NHS trust and one HEI for one course. All are set within a framework of guidance determined by the Department of Health (DoH) and the appropriate professional governing body.

This chapter concentrates on those relationships surrounding nursing, midwifery and, to a lesser extent, allied health disciplines. Medicine is traditionally somewhat different with the medical school frequently being much more autonomous within a university than a faculty of health. However, this difference has been eroded over the past decade, with the recognition of the growing need for library services able to serve a broad health client group (Hewlett, 1992). This need resulted in an NHS Guidance Note (NHS Executive, 1997) about libraries in hospitals, which acknowledges that 'all staff [should] have access to a multidisciplinary library and that it is the role of NHS Trusts to draw up a library and information strategy covering all staff groups'. The libraries run by universities to support medical schools are, therefore, now frequently delivering services to both doctors and other health professionals.

It is clear that, despite the history of medical libraries being somewhat different, many of the issues surrounding relationships between HE and the NHS are common to the provision of any library services for health and the reader should find useful pointers regardless of perspective.

The education of nurses

In 1986 the United Kingdom Central Council for Nursing, Midwifery and Health Visiting (UKCC) published its vision for the future education and training of nurses, known as Project 2000. This heralded the move away from independent nursing schools to contracted agreements for nurse education to be delivered by HEIs. Project 2000 presented HE libraries with a range of challenges; in many ways these were similar to the challenges described in Chapter 6, but magnified on an instant and grand scale with student numbers of over 300 per year. Often with multiple intakes and with entry criteria less than for the traditional first-degree entrant, the students would spend time both in their HEI and in a local hospital trust for a clinical placement. The local hospitals generally had some of the resources the students needed, but previously may not have considered nurses to be part of their client base; the old colleges of nursing had resources but were not on the scale now required and they might not be available to all the new students. The result was that, in order to cope with the projected numbers generated by Project 2000, HEIs had to build their collections rapidly in new subject areas and work in partnership with the NHS.

Miers (2002) documents some of the cultural challenges presented as nursing moved towards receiving equal status with other academic disciplines and highlights the importance of two documents that both confirmed the continued role of HEIs working in partnership with the NHS. *Fitness for Practice* (UKCC, 1999) confirmed the position of nurse education in HEIs while strengthening the links with practice through contracts between the then Workforce Development Confederations and HEIs for pre- and post-registration education. *Making a Difference* (DoH, 1999) set out a new model of nursing education that would include greater flexibility, widening access and increased recruitment, thus introducing the challenging elements discussed in Chapter 6. In addition, for the HE–NHS partnership, the model introduced a shift away from the HEI with longer placements heralding greater demands on the NHS library services. At the other end of the information spectrum, there are references to the importance of research and evidence-based practice, which again reinforce the need for successful working partnerships between HEIs and the NHS.

Library resources

In 2001 the University Health Sciences Librarians group (UHSL) and the Library and Information Co-operation Council (LINC) Health Panel (now known as HELICON) commissioned a review of the impact of *Making a Difference* on HE libraries (Gannon-Leary, Wakeham and Walton, 2003). This identifies 63 HEIs with nurse education and a 50% increase in student nursing numbers in the six years since 1995. The report describes an increasingly diverse pattern of delivery with more time being spent in the clinical areas, greater support for evidence-based practice and many more appointments of lecturer practitioners, who not only act as a bridge between HE and the NHS but also have need themselves for good library services in both locations. The ability of HEIs to deliver support at a distance has been enhanced by schemes such as UK Libraries Plus and by electronic access, but, with the 'step on step off' concept of continuing professional development, care is needed to identify who is eligible for what, when and where. These issues are all common to the HE–FE agenda as well, but with the added complexity of multiple contracts issued by the NHS. There is also an apparent lack of certainty that funding within the NHS trusts is always appropriately reaching the trust library services, limiting their ability to function in any partnership with HE.

Development is still required for robust partnerships to exist at all levels, not least because of the importance of ensuring effective contribution to the multidisciplinary agenda with its latest requirement for common inter-professional units that will empower the student to work within both HE and NHS environments from the moment they begin training.

The hoped-for changes may have been slow to appear, partly because of organizational barriers raised by the frequent reorganizations of the NHS. History would suggest that there will continue to be shifts and changes in negotiating and funding HEIs to deliver education and training for the NHS.

NHS library policy

In 2004, TFPL Ltd was commissioned by the NHS to review NHS library policy. The resulting report (Herman and Ward, 2004) includes a statement that suggests there still is a long way to go to achieve close operational partnerships between HE and the NHS, a challenge that is dominated by the problems of accessing electronic resources under the restrictive licences discussed in earlier chapters. The extract that follows is potentially a seminal statement in the history of HE and NHS partnerships:

> Access to knowledge is needed by health and social care staff and students who need to move between NHS and HE locations. Contracts for library services provide some services but many users, including consultants, researchers and students, find their need for information is restricted by the terms of licences for electronic content. The *Users First* report commissioned by the NHS and Higher Education has identified what needs to be done to simplify and improve services for users and has prioritised projects to achieve the required change. Partnership working across the NHS UK wide and with Higher Education, Further Education and public libraries will be increasingly important in helping NHS staff and patients to gain access to the information they need. (15)

There does, however, appear to be a glaring omission from the picture of partnership – that is the emergence of the NHS University (NHSU). In the summer of 2004 the NHSU described itself as a new kind of learning organization providing learning and development opportunities for everyone working in health and social care. Much of the early work has been on a framework for foundation degrees, which has immediately brought FE into the HE–NHS partnership. The NHSU website (2003a) declares its intention to:

Not duplicate existing provision, or compete unnecessarily with established providers. Instead, as well as developing our own learning programmes, we will act as brokers for existing facilities, resources and provision, adapting them where necessary. We are already working with universities and colleges to deliver our first learning programmes, and discussing roll-out and future developments with others.

At a point of apparent consolidation of approach being outlined in *Users First* (Thornhill, 2003) and the *NHS Library Policy Review* (Herman and Ward, 2004), the NHS is also establishing NHSU, thus suggesting that HEIs will be part, but not the only part, of future NHS partnerships to deliver education and training.

Establishing the relationship

Although many informal schemes between HEIs and the NHS were developed within the Project 2000 contract groupings, the vision of seamless and simply funded access to use any library is still unfulfilled. The following are examples of some best-practice case studies. What determines the approach is the contractual context, the experiences of previous attempts at partnership, and the clarity of and confidence in the arrangements being proposed by the HEI responsible for delivering the contract.

As with HE in FE, there is a danger that the HEI will be perceived as Big Brother, or even as Scrooge, with presumed wealth but a disinclination to distribute it to the NHS trust libraries that are required to support the students. This can lead to resentment and misunderstanding about responsibilities. Poor communication resulting from geographical remoteness, lack of time and lack of co-ordination can aggravate the situation and lead to further misunderstandings.

The complexity of funding streams within the NHS has led to many trust libraries fighting for service-level agreements with their different client groups. This may work for some HE–NHS partnerships, where the relationship can be simply articulated and agreed by both parties. However, the relationship between one HEI and the NHS commissioning agent may have many different strands and may lead to students coming from many different trusts and undergoing placements in several other trusts. Close working partnerships with all the NHS trusts that may have students on placement will facilitate an open approach. Perhaps a service-level statement that articulates what any student can expect is the most productive form of agreement, especially if it also provides the foundation for quality enhancement. The concept of a passport to enable students to move between libraries, as study and the clinical placement require, was favoured in the early 1990s (Beard, 1995).

Communication

The best-practice approach for establishing channels of communication outlined in Chapter 6 should be adopted, and adapted where necessary to reflect the dual responsibilities that trusts have to their employees while they are also students. Since several trusts will frequently be involved in supporting students on one course, it can be beneficial for them to meet together with the HEI subject specialists and service managers to foster common approaches. The best partnership meetings will also have representation from academics and managers responsible for contracts. These meetings should be recorded and actions noted and subsequently reported.

The ultimate version of establishing relationships, by jointly planning and delivering a new multidisciplinary service, may sometimes be appropriate. Edge Hill College of Higher Education has pioneered such an approach (Black and Bury, 2004). The project concentrated on improving service by rationalizing in one location and by working on a collaborative vision of resource funding, access and development. An alternative model is to develop a service to a locality or region; one such example in the north-east of England was also based on collaborative working described as a 'mosaic of access solutions', which require 'the creation of a self-sustaining partnership independent of the presence of specific individuals and robust in a climate of change' (Childs and Banwell, 2001). Whether delivery is through a consolidated service or a federal approach the partnerships should follow jointly agreed principles.

A review by Crawford (2002) of the Glasgow Caledonian experience highlights more points to consider when establishing relationships. He articulates something that will strike a chord with any librarian who has worked with nursing students: 'nursing students rely more heavily on the library than other stakeholder groups' (91). There is also reference to a difference in culture already familiar from the discussion of FE: HE encourages students to develop the ability to locate and use information independently, while NHS services tend to provide the information. This can give the impression to the user that the NHS library is more user-focused than its HE counterpart.

Not all the relationships will be with NHS trusts; increasingly placement opportunities will involve primary care. In a review of support for general practice, Gillies (2000, 95) comments: 'a doctor's information system [which can be viewed as] a collection of rooms within a virtual library, illustrates quite clearly that simply stepping into a physical library building does not provide information on its own . . . Users of the library, physical or virtual, require directions, guidance and training in the devices provided.'

Training and support

This view, if shared between the HE and NHS sectors, should provide an excellent opportunity for developing the training required. Both sectors have experience in different aspects of training. HEIs have expertise in mass education; the NHS has excellence in the area of supporting critical appraisal; both have expertise in supporting research. With the introduction of the National Electronic Library for Health (NeLH) and its core content, librarians in the NHS have had extensive opportunities to develop their knowledge of resources and have needed to develop their training skills to support their users. HE library staff may still have broader experience of resources and multiple interfaces, but together it should be possible to ensure that the health student acquires the appropriate information literacy skills to function, whatever the search platform they might encounter.

Peripatetic support is another area where both sectors have begun to gain experience. The NHS has employed library professionals to move out from lead NHS trust libraries to support the development of skills by users in remote locations, including primary care. The focus has been on the development of appropriate IT and information literacy skills. HEIs should continue to develop the concept outlined in the previous chapter, to enable the communication and support across the large number of placement and teaching environments that will form part of the contract portfolio of the HEI.

Strategic management

How can librarians who find themselves responsible for providing services to the NHS establish what the current constraints may be? The biggest ally in this must be the HE staff member responsible for the NHS contracts, who will be able to describe what has been agreed. A continuing exchange of information should facilitate the library's responsiveness to changes in funding streams or new contracts and influence the type of service to be articulated in future agreements.

Management

Once a relationship has been established, it requires continuing management at the strategic level if it is to be effective. With the high levels of both theory and practice it is advisable to maintain close links, perhaps through the formulation of a review group, not only with contract managers or fund holders and senior library managers, but also with senior academics and lecturer practitioners. Library services need to be represented at a strategic level in the wider institutional context and senior library staff should be members of relevant committees in both the HEI and the NHS. With different stakeholders involved a clear management structure should be agreed (Black and Bury, 2004, 42).

Co-ordination of services is essential, especially where one HEI has several NHS partners. These individual relationships should be viewed as a single network and, where possible, decisions should be made that are appropriate across the network. This enables the HEI to ensure an equitable level of service to all its students; within the HE and NHS context this is increasingly by means of electronic resources. It also permits libraries within the network to share experience, knowledge and information. As with FECs, NHS libraries should know what they need to achieve but must be allowed the flexibility to implement services in a way that best suits their service. In 2003 it was identified that, of the 42 respondents to the SCONUL survey of funding to support the NHS, 67% had some form of service-level agreement and 46% were formula-driven; 69% of the contracts had been established since 1995 and 26% since 2000 (SCONUL Advisory Committee on Health Sciences, 2003). Standards are essential but must accommodate diversity.

As with HE in FE, when a network consists of a number of libraries, it is easy to lose sight of the overall picture. The co-ordination of services, therefore, needs to be allocated to an individual librarian with strategic responsibilities. Given the rapid and continuing changes within the NHS, it is vital that the librarian develop contacts that will allow them to understand the prevailing NHS strategy and culture; it is equally important to reciprocate with their NHS colleagues to impart knowledge of developments in HE.

In a similar vein, it is vital that students are enabled to exploit the resources provided by both their HE library and the appropriate NHS library. As the employment destination for the majority of the students is likely to include access to the National Library for Health (NLH) – the proposed expansion of the NeLH portal to all relevant health information – it is critical that the learning experience incorporate both the HE route to information and familiarity with the NLH view.

The *Users First* report (Thornhill, 2003) articulates some still prevalent misunderstandings. On the one hand, academics can feel that the NHS will receive high levels of library provision from HE at uneconomic rates with risks of high demand and volume of use. On the other hand, the NHS perception is sometimes of restriction, especially of access to electronic resources, caused by a lack of understanding of what the licences and funding might provide.

Planning

When planning services, libraries need to take into account the unique nature of the courses and the students. The evidence-based and flexible delivery agenda, with its emphasis on continuing professional development, was articulated in *Making a Difference* (DoH, 1999). This requires close partnerships not only between libraries but between those designing the courses and those commissioning them at the local level. It may also be important to be aware of the role the NHSU might play in any course procurement process.

Libraries also need to be involved at a strategic level in the planning process for new courses. If they are not involved at an early stage, it may be impossible to provide adequate resources to meet the course plan. It is the responsibility of the HE library staff to participate in this process, but close involvement of the NHS partners should enhance the outcome. Most course validations will involve practitioners and the future purchasers of the course. If there is to be an off-campus location for all the taught components, then the managers of that service must be closely involved. With the growth of foundation degrees in health, the partnership with the NHS will also need to include HE in FE partnerships: all the advice given in Chapter 6 will apply.

Funding

It has long been recognized, for instance by Capel, Banwell and Walton (1997), that funding is of paramount importance and as yet is not regularized. This can have a significant impact on the decision-making process. For example, an NHS trust that has not been receiving funding for its library service from within the NHS will be unable to provide the expected services to students when they arrive on clinical placement. The HEI will have been funded to provide resources for the educational process, which includes hard-copy and electronic resources, but will probably not have been resourced to contribute to the basic infrastructure needed to operate the trust service. It is expected that proposed reforms of the way HEIs receive their money from the NHS, and the corresponding reforms to the way the NHS libraries are funded, should lead to the long awaited transparency. Thornhill (2003) suggests that the Multi-Professional Education and Training (MPET) budget may contribute to better transparency and he places great importance on the value of the core electronic content negotiated by the NHS as another part of the funding solution. However, this will be dependent on successful negotiation with publishers, who currently derive important income from sales to both HE and NHS markets. It is too early to say if a reasonable single procurement can be achieved that avoids duplication and recognizes the right to have access at a rate acceptable to both purchaser and vendor. Solutions will need strategic negotiation at the highest level and the library manager will have to keep abreast of the developments. As reported by Herman and Ward (2004), the developments will need to be at both national and local levels.

Regardless of the method of funding, HEI and NHS library staff have to work together to ensure adequate budgets. HE student numbers will include large cohorts of pre-registration nursing students and small numbers on some specialized post-experience courses; the resources, particularly journals and e-books, are expensive. Consortium purchasing, well established in both HE and NHS cultures, offers some leverage on price. Electronic resources will grow in importance, in the form of both monographs and serials; these are expensive, but highly appropriate, given the dispersed nature of the student group. NHS–HE contracts are increasingly based on a low unit price per student; this will present a significant challenge to those trying to broker effective procurement deals.

The NHSU publicity provides a useful conclusion to the discussion of strategic issues. In 2003 the NHS was investing £3 billion in education and training for its staff, the largest spend of any employer in Europe. It is not clear what the impact on the HE–NHS partnership will be, but the strategic plan gives a clear multi-professional and interdisciplinary focus with a commitment to quality and equity (NHSU, 2003b); these issues must influence the HE–NHS strategic agenda.

Service provision

Effective local service provision, whether in the HEI or the NHS placement, has three key elements: resources, training and services.

Resources

Hard-copy resources are generally provided in both libraries with funds that are currently provided through the HEIs from the monies received under the contract with the NHS. This is one area of funding that should be streamlined in the future, with the money for the NHS part of the support going directly to the NHS library.

Online resources are provided by the HEI through the library's website and increasingly the faculty VLE. Although the NHS libraries may have space for students to study, and frequently 24-hour reference access, there can still be a relative lack of accessible IT facilities with connection to the HE network. HEIs have the responsibility to ensure that their students can access their networks, and so will frequently fund IT facilities; but these, while providing good access to the HEI learning resources, are then not providing the access that the NHS trust employee experiences. This limits the ability of NHS librarians to provide day-to-day help and support. Many students will study both in their HEI and in the clinical placement setting and so, unlike their HE in FE counterparts, have realistic opportunities to use libraries in both locations. However, this can lead to an over-reliance on the HEI library providing all the support and training.

There are also challenges surrounding the licensing of the information. Before the NeLH developments, and particularly before the introduction of the NHS-wide procurement of a core content collection available to all NHS and private health-care organizations, HEIs were the only realistic providers of electronic information to those studying health-care disciplines. Now, although HE may still have a wider range, the strategic issues are about ensuring appropriate licences to enable single authenticated log-in regardless of where the accredited user may be. Currently it is quite possible for an individual to have legitimate access to the NHS core content and to the HE collection; both will have been paid for but they will have different authentication.

As previously mentioned, the NHS libraries now have access to the core content deal, which provides a significant overlap in resource availability. However, there are currently two subscriptions, licences and password processes and often different physical computers to be used. This leads to inevitable frustrations and misunderstandings about what can legitimately be used and by whom. The HEI may well grant honorary teaching staff status to the lecturer practitioner and so enable them to access the university's resources, but the mentors who work with the students may be denied this access. Conversely, students who are NHS employees will have access to the NHS system but other health-care students may not.

Although health education is driven by the concepts of evidence-based and reflective practice, academic staff may not appreciate the problems of access to electronic resources or providing appropriate print resources. It is not unknown for programmes of study to be moved from one teaching location to another and for it to be assumed that the printed resources previously used by the course can be as easily relocated. Rarely will this be economic and both the NHS, HEI and, increasingly, FEC librarians may have to work together to make the case for new provision and for this to be electronic provision whenever possible.

Training

There is an obvious challenge for any training in use of the e-resources to cover both HE and NHS systems; this can be overcome by developing a collaborative programme. The HE contract may be predicated on the HEI providing the in-depth training within the university; however, only the NHS can provide the training associated with the NHS core content. One way forward is to work on the common transferable skills supporting information literacy. The programmes can therefore be developed together and delivered on different platforms without redundancy or unnecessary duplication. The information literacy agenda is one of the targets outlined in *Users First* (Thornhill, 2003). The development of inter-professional education units for all health courses should give opportunity for information literacy skills to be embedded in the curriculum and potentially avoid them being seen as an optional extra by the student. It is important, therefore, for librarians from both the HEIs and the clinical placement settings to be involved in the content development of these units.

One difficulty inherent in delivering training to health-care student groups is the wide range of abilities within each individual group. Like HE in FE students, they tend to come from a wide range of backgrounds and so have different educational experiences and different levels of competence. Many health faculties have programmes for developing students' ICT skills and any library programmes should ideally be timed to follow the acquisition of these skills. It will still be necessary to have help-desk support, drop-in follow-up sessions or self-directed materials for some students to follow.

Services

The development of health faculty VLE pages can provide an excellent catalyst for increasing the take-up of electronic resources, with links to both e-journals and e-books embedded in electronic reading lists. Finding faculty learning and teaching champions will make a difference to how the challenge of resource acquisition, training and access can be resolved.

Partnerships may want to use an interactive information skills programme as part of what is offered through the VLE; they may want to incorporate an electronic enquiry service to support the students not on campus. An added advantage of VLEs is that they may enable library staff to work more closely with academic colleagues and so enhance awareness of the library's contribution to the learning process.

One strength of health education is that nursing and midwifery teaching staff have long been required to have teaching qualifications. New entrants will often now be taking programmes with e-learning modules as part of the curriculum. When looking for champions to increase the integration of learning resources into the VLE and the curriculum, the newly qualified may be some of the most receptive to the concept of blended learning. Externally funded projects or high-profile national initiatives may also be a lure, with the prospect of enhanced reputation for the individual and the faculty and institution. The substantial health contracts are vital to the economic stability of the HEIs and the added value of innovative learning resource initiatives should not be underestimated.

A positive advantage of the HE–NHS partnership is that students should find libraries increasingly available 24 hours a day, seven days a week. The NHS has always provided this self-service approach for the medics and HEIs are now introducing self-service technologies; electronic resources of course obviate the need to enter the physical library at all. The use of both HEI and NHS libraries by most students does mean that all library staff need to be aware that the nature of the individual support they provide should contribute to fostering evidence-based and reflective practice and should complement and not contradict the advice they might receive in the other half of the partnership.

Quality assurance

Quality assurance of health education courses and library provision has in the past had almost as many strands as the funding. It is, therefore, a well established part of the culture of both HE and the NHS. Until recently, however, all had to cope with multiple and overlapping processes, which were often diametrically opposed (Hewlett and Walton, 2001). Accreditation fatigue has been a very real phenomenon, with much emphasis on data gathering at the expense of actually enhancing services. However, as with funding, real progress is being made. The DoH (England), in partnership with the Nursing and Midwifery Council, the Health Professions Council and the contracting bodies within the NHS, has agreed that the Quality Assurance Agency (QAA) should carry out 'reviews of all NHS-funded healthcare programmes in England during the period 2003–2006' (QAA, 2003). The handbook for review makes the following comment:

> [T]he DoH has an interest in bringing key stakeholders together to provide assurance that programmes produce practitioners who are safe and competent to practise and who are equipped to work in a patient-centred NHS. The quality assurance arrangements should build on the internal quality assurance of healthcare education providers and make best use of existing documentation and data.

HEI and placement partner libraries need to work together to prepare their self-evaluation document (SED). The document allows an evaluation of what they do and why, and how they fulfil their aims. In this review cycle there is a tripartite arrangement, with the reviewers looking at whether the education is fit for practice (the responsibility of the Professional Statutory and Regulatory Bodies (PSRBs)), for purpose (the commissioning bodies) and for the award (the responsibility of the HEIs). In common with other QAA review processes there will be an expectation of evidence of student involvement in the production of the SED and in this case also the practitioners. Librarians need to work together to ensure their early involvement in the planning process and to present both the strengths, with evidence, and any weaknesses, with plans for improvements articulated. The HEI partner will have considerable experience in the process of developmental audit and can therefore share this culture with their NHS colleagues, who will be used to a service audit where more weight is given to the provision of services than to the evidence of quality enhancement at work.

This quality assurance and enhancement approach is not in conflict with the accreditation process now increasingly used within the NHS. HEIs need to put in place quality assurance systems that can be used across their network of NHS partners. These systems need to take into account the differences between individual libraries and also to ensure an appropriate standard of service.

Reference is made in Chapter 6 to the adaptation by Bournemouth University of the LINC Health Panel accreditation tool for use with its FEC partner colleges. The LINC Health Panel tool has now been updated by HELICON, the successor organization, and is rapidly becoming the standard accreditation tool for the NHS. This means that HEIs do not need to carry out accreditation themselves to ensure that an NHS trust has an appropriate library service able to support its HE students; rather the focus can be on an annual monitoring of a framework for continuing quality enhancement. This process can relate to any specific contracted partnerships, agreements or service-level statements. It should include the gathering and use of qualitative feedback from staff and students. The documentation from this evaluative and supportive process will then be available as evidence for QAA audit and should see year-on-year improvement to the library services provided by the HEI and NHS to the accredited HE students.

Documentation is important evidence for QAA reviews and the involvement of librarians in important quality assurance events, such as course review and validation, not only helps ensure appropriate development of the learning resources but also enhances the likelihood of good investment in resources and a positive comment in any QAA review. As has been previously mentioned, positive reports from the QAA's major review of health care will be vital to the HEI seeking contracts from the NHS.

It is also incumbent on HE librarians to increase the engagement of their NHS colleagues in this quality enhancement agenda. This may be achieved in part through their own positions on HEI deliberative committees or participation in HEI quality enhancement processes. It has been suggested that a consultative or review committee be formed to discuss strategic resource and service development issues and that this group should also consider quality review. The committee should report on the HEI deliberative structure and should have robust processes to track actions and responses. The membership should represent all partner libraries, the academics and those with contract responsibilities.

External partnerships

With the growth of foundation degrees it has already been suggested that the HE–NHS partnership will increasingly involve FECs. The *NHS Library Policy Review* also points up the importance of partnerships with public libraries (Herman and Ward, 2004). However, perhaps the most important new partnership is the one between the NHSU and the HEIs. This might also involve HEIs collaborating with commercial training organizations. The invitations to tender may, in an echo of HEFCE strategy discussed in Chapter 1, increasingly involve HEIs working together within regions rather than in competition.

There will be continuing partnerships with the PSRBs and there may be a need to develop programmes at sub-degree level for health-care assistants and others. In order to share best practice and help develop new ways of collaborating, it will be important to continue to utilize or take part in the work of special interest groups such as the CILIP Health Libraries Group, UHSL, the University Medical School Librarians Group and the NHS/HE Forum.

Conclusions

The relationship between HEI and NHS libraries should be a strengthening one, primarily because of the long awaited strategic rationalization of NHS funding and the development of the NLH. The increasing commonalities between HE and NHS cultures in supporting evidence-based practice should also encourage partnership; however, the culture of mass HE is still very different from the research-oriented clinical effectiveness agenda.

There may be some challenges ahead as the NLH gathers momentum. There would appear to be a risk that local NHS trust librarians might feel disenfranchised by the emergence of the NLH as the source of all information and this could bring a tension into their local relationships with the HEI. HEIs may feel constrained by what might be available in any core content deal they have access to.

The development of the HE–NHS partnerships will therefore need flexibility and sensitivity to ensure continued quality of service to the students, particularly if the service is increasingly based on electronic resources. The relationship should be led by a senior staff member in both the HEI and the NHS.

For electronic services to be developed successfully there will need to be new cross-sector procurement agreements with publishers, a rationalization of the licence arrangements and movement to cross-sector access to networks.

The emergence of robust VLEs should facilitate remote access but will also require new partnerships to deliver the information literacy skills and support needed if the student is to become an evidence-based practitioner. The skills acquired will also need to equip the student to work in both the HE and NHS environments.

Librarians will need to be closely involved in any tenders and contracts so that best practice for learning resources is incorporated within the wider value-for-money educational framework. Clarity will still be required to identify roles and responsibilities, but this can be through a service-level agreement or statement. Quality assurance should continue to stress the value of enhancement which can best be achieved by continuing to work in partnership.

Finally, it remains to be seen how the role of the NHSU might affect the HE–NHS relationship.

8
Library collaboration: the regional/national dimension and project working

Introduction

Collaboration has been endemic to libraries since the days when copyists travelled between them. National initiatives are often led by overarching bodies, such as the JISC. However, as far as the individual library is concerned, collaboration is often characterized by its regional nature and by receipt of project funding. These two dimensions are the foci of this chapter.

Collaboration

Useful definitions of the various levels of what may generally be termed collaboration are offered by the report *Barriers to Resource Sharing among Higher Education Libraries* (Higher Education Consultancy Group and CHEMS Consulting, 2002). In ascending order of the level of commitment, these are:

- **Co-ordination** – a general process involving communication and consultation
- **Co-operation** – a basic level of working together, in that without co-operation nothing can be achieved
- **Collaboration** – joint working, which involves a conscious and shared approach planning, implementing and reviewing aspects of library services, but not necessarily the commitment of any significant resources
- **Partnership** – a more formal and explicit approach to collaboration, often involving key roles and responsibilities being determined at the outset

- **Resource sharing** – forms of working with other libraries that, by definition, involve the sharing of resources, whether finance, staffing, services, accommodation and infrastructural support, or collections
- **Deep resource sharing** – collaboration between or among libraries in which institutional autonomy in service provision is in some degree surrendered, and which involves some degree of risk.

Co-ordination and co-operation permeate academic, and most other, libraries; collaboration and partnership are widespread, often involving formal agreements between institutions; resource sharing, at either level, is less common, involving as it does some degree of lost autonomy on the part of individual intuitions. All levels of collaboration offer benefits to the participants; it may be argued that resource sharing brings the greatest benefits in terms of efficiency and return on investment, but is the most difficult to achieve.

Regional collaboration often implies a cross-sectoral approach – working across the various library sectors, such as HE, FE, public and special libraries. Increasingly it also involves a cross-domain approach – working across the domains of libraries, museums and archives that are brought together in national bodies such as the Museums, Libraries and Archives Council (MLA) and Museums, Archives and Libraries Wales (CyMAL).

The regional dimension

Chapters 6 and 7 on relationships with FE and the NHS provide some good illustrations of the importance of the regional dimension for academic libraries. Consider Staff Nurse Terry, who is an example, drawn from life, of the work-based distance learner. Terry works in a hospital and therefore has access to the hospital library; Terry is enrolled on an HE course delivered in the local FEC, and uses both the HEI's resources (chiefly electronic) and the FEC's library; Terry lives within five minutes' walk of a good-sized public library, and uses it not only for leisure reading but also for access to the internet through the People's Network. Terry's use of libraries in pursuit of a professional qualification is not limited to or constrained by affiliation to the HEI; to provide a service matching Terry's needs and pattern of usage, the home HEI must have good co-operative relationships with the other libraries in the region served.

The regional focus is not merely pragmatic: as is evident in the discussion of the HE context in Chapter 1, the government and the UK funding councils for HE are increasingly giving a regional dimension to strategy. HEFCE's annual review for 2002/3 (HEFCE, 2003b, 17), for instance, recognizes the growing significance of the English regions for economic and social regeneration and the importance of every region offering 'the full range of HE services – teaching, research, support for business and the community, and opportunities for a wide range of students'. Regional consortia of HEIs are seen as having 'a central role in co-ordinating collaborative activity, and in linking with regional partners outside the sector'; the role of FECs in joint working and the co-ordination of courses offered is also recognized. HEFCE itself has regional teams, dealing with many HE matters.

This emerging regional structure is mirrored among the HEIs: in England, there is one association of HEIs covering each of the nine regions. These were created in response partly to HEFCE's emphasis on regionalism, partly to the growing powers and importance of regional structures – Government Offices, Regional Development Agencies and Regional Assemblies.

This section deals with libraries' response to and place in the regional structures in England. It also covers the sub-UK national dimension. The other home countries (Northern Ireland, Scotland and Wales) are similar to the English regions in terms of numbers of HEIs and sometimes geographic area too: Scotland has 20 HEIs and Wales 14 (*Higher Education in the United Kingdom*, 2004); North West and South West England have 15 and 13 respectively (HEFCE, 2003b) and have an area similar to that of Wales. The home countries, of course, are different, with nation status and varying degrees of devolution not yet evident in England. However, the similarity of scale warrants this joint consideration.

Drivers and challenges

The drivers for and challenges of regional collaboration have been analysed as part of the Welsh Higher Education Libraries Forum's (WHELF) Higher Education Libraries in Partnership (HELP) Project (Kensler, 2004). While some elements may seem unique to Wales, such as geography, the majority of the issues are common to academic libraries elsewhere. The analysis will therefore serve as a useful framework for a discussion of regional collaboration.

The drivers for regional collaboration within individual institutions include improving users' access; sharing expertise and identifying good practice; reducing duplication of effort; consortial funding bids. There is also a strategic dimension, emanating from the National Assembly for Wales and the Higher Education Funding Council for Wales (HEFCW), but shared in large measure by the other UK funding councils. The strategic drivers for Wales are resonant of those discussed in Chapter 1 and include reconfiguration and collaboration; strengthening research through joint action; excellence in teaching and learning; widening access; efficiency gains; supporting lifelong learning. There is also an intensifying national and international climate fostering collaboration, as evidenced by such bodies and initiatives as the Research Support Libraries Programme (RSLP), the Wider Libraries Programme (WILIP) consultation exercise and the (then) Library Association's Lifelong Learning Strategy.

Another strong driver is the increasing identification of English government with the regions. While this has always been the case in the other home nations, it is a new development in England, and a trend intensified throughout the UK by devolution. The Museums, Libraries and Archives Council (MLA), a non-departmental public body funded by the Department for Culture, Media and Sport (DCMS), has set up Museums, Libraries and Archives Councils for each of the English regions. The MLA's remit, replicated in those of the regional councils, is to provide leadership, advocacy and advice for the three domains. In its first years of operation from its formation in 2000, the MLA's focus was on the public library sector: public libraries are the statutory responsibility of the MLA's parent body, the DCMS; HE and other libraries are not within the DCMS's remit. However, in 2002 the MLA set up the Wider Information and Library Issues Project (WILIP, now expanded to the Wider Libraries Programme) to ensure that the MLA (then Resource) was 'sufficiently engaged with the non-public library parts of the library and information world' (Howley and Stevens, 2003). The main issues identified were improved user access, funding and sustainability of initiatives, workforce development, developing a strategic framework, and advocacy. These issues, which provide the focus for the regional councils as well as the MLA, will clearly have an impact on HE libraries and will offer another strong justification for HE libraries to develop a robust regional identity.

The challenges of regional collaboration include:

- the staff resource needed to co-ordinate, support and drive forward co-operation and collaboration
- geography
- the diversity of institutions, which may have very different user-bases, some focusing on learning/teaching, others on research
- competition between institutions
- the involvement of different sectors, particularly the NHS
- lack of awareness of strategies and initiatives among all staff of an institution

- failure to identify and communicate the benefits to all staff of an institution
- the identification of income streams with individual institutions or indeed individual departments
- the perception that collaboration may undermine income generation
- the feeling that larger issues such as licensing and authentication need to be addressed at a higher (UK-wide) level.

Some of these challenges have to do with culture and communication within institutions. The high-level strategic priority now placed by funding bodies on collaboration should eventually help to bring about cultural change and diminish these. Others are more fundamental. Geography is particularly inhibiting in Wales, but can be equally problematic in Scotland and some of the larger English regions such as the South West. It can be difficult to find commonalities between universities that have large and almost exclusively undergraduate populations and those that are focused on research. Conversely, the HEIs focused mainly on teaching may see themselves as competing with each other for relatively scarce student numbers, although the practice of 'co-opetition' (competing businesses collaborating where it is in their financial interests, such as lumber companies in Scandinavia running a common transport system) is widespread in the commercial world.

The strength of the challenges and the general lack of strong corporate drivers have in the main led to collaboration being confined to the levels of co-ordination or co-operation.

Areas for collaboration

The HELP *Collaboration Review* (Kensler, 2004) also identifies four main areas for regional collaboration. These are:

- **Collection management** – includes activities such as improved resource discovery, collaborative purchasing and collection management, deep resource sharing, and shared storage
- **Service provision** – includes interlending and document supply, and reciprocal borrowing and access schemes
- **Training and other staff activities** – include collaborative staff development and information skills programmes, and disaster planning
- **Technical areas** – such as shared systems and MLEs/VLEs.

The rest of this section addresses each area in turn, with some examples of actual collaboration.

Collection management – journals

The *Final Report* (2003) of the Research Support Libraries Group (RSLG) urges 'a concerted shift from the comparatively loose network of providers, each servicing its own user group, to a more coherently managed network in which providers work together to develop and deliver an agreed national agenda'. The collections of individual HEIs and the national libraries are seen as a single resource that should in the future be managed on a more collaborative basis.

Given the comparative under-performance of research in Wales and the importance of journals in supporting research, the HELP Project undertook a case study to establish the practicality and feasibility of such collaborative collection management of journals (Kensler et al., 2004). Published statistics showed Welsh HEIs spending roughly 20% of total library budgets, or 50% of their information budgets, on journals; the expenditure on journal subscriptions had increased by an average of 40% over the previous six years, compared with an average increase of 16% in total library budgets. The case study estimated that a total of 31,764 print journal titles were available in the Welsh HEIs; of these a surprising 25,070 (or 79%) were unique to single institutions.

Given the extent of spending on journals and the number of unique titles, the study concludes that resource discovery needs to be improved, so that HE researchers know where titles are available, for instance through a union list, as do promotion of existing access schemes.

The number of electronic titles and expenditure on them are growing in Wales as everywhere else. The study interestingly concludes that a collaborative approach to purchasing these should also be investigated to explore whether additional cost benefits could be gained over and above the pricing negotiated nationally. There were indications that some publishers might be amenable to approaches from formal or informal consortia of libraries: by purchasing jointly, individual libraries might gain access at a reduced price to collections they would not purchase; publishers would increase revenue by accepting fractional subscriptions that would otherwise not be paid.

The Welsh HEIs collectively have a growing storage problem for journals. Buying in electronic format does not necessarily enable libraries to discard the print version; many titles are not available or subscribed to in electronic form. An innovative approach to this problem has been taken in Scotland by HE libraries and the National Library of Scotland (NLS) (Nicholson, 2004). It is worth examining the Scottish experience in some detail, since it illustrates what is achievable.

Building on a long tradition of collaboration, which includes the Conspectus exercise in the 1980s (Ball, 1987) and the Scottish Collections Network (SCONE), funding was obtained in 2001 for a study of the feasibility of setting up a Collaborative Academic Store for Scotland (CASS). The study established the need for CASS and proposed models of ownership and operation. A bid for funding to the Scottish Higher Education Funding Council (SHEFC) was unsuccessful. However, the need was becoming more and more intense, with little prospect of capital for new library buildings. An immediate solution was offered by the NLS, in the form of secure storage space and 12,000 m of compact shelving at one of its sites in Edinburgh. Seven HEIs are participating, with collections of both journals and monographs of various sizes. Records of the stock are held on individual OPACs and as a separate readily available CASS database. Access to the stock is mediated by NLS staff, through delivery to the NLS reading room, to the home library or by photocopy or fax.

While CASS in its present form does not meet all the needs identified in the feasibility study, it is providing much needed off-site storage for unused materials. It is also evidence of strong partnership and commitment between a range of diverse partners, and of strategic thinking about and collaboration on collections and services. The level of commitment, together with the development of a working model and the demonstration of concrete benefits, augur well for future bids for funding.

Collection management – collaborative purchasing

In the UK, purchasing consortia, as Chapter 4 demonstrates, are an accepted and integral part of collaboration. They also have a strong regional basis, which may not, however, map to the established regional and national structure in the UK: NEYAL (North East and Yorkshire Academic Libraries), for instance, spans two of the English regions, the North East and Yorkshire and the Humber. Their focus has tended to be on purchasing agreements, which their members then use to buy what they will. There has been little if any collaborative purchasing through these structures, in the sense of collective decision-making on what individual libraries will buy or specialize in.

The North American consortia, such as OhioLink, operate differently. Electronic resources may be bought by the consortium on behalf of its members, not as in the UK by the individual libraries. There is also a trend to taking a consortial view of monograph purchases, facilitated by suppliers that have developed such a view of what is being purchased through their systems. YBP, for instance, offers each member library the option of viewing all purchases of any title by other consortium members. Spending decisions can then be made in the light of what is available for loan in other libraries, with underlying agreements on levels of holdings. This has the potential to bring savings and maximize the effectiveness of financial resources.

This trend is now becoming evident in the UK in the collaborative purchase of e-books, with NoWAL (North West Academic Libraries) leading the way. NoWAL is a consortium of 15 HEIs, which grew from CALIM (Consortium of Academic Libraries in Manchester), a very close-knit consortium with a small geographic spread, supported by an ethos of close collaboration at vice-chancellor level. It is in some ways different from the other regional purchasing consortia in the UK, since it can be seen as the product of a commitment to collaboration rather than of a pragmatic need to save money.

NoWAL has developed a three-year agreement with NetLibrary for 12 of its members, providing 12,000 copyright titles and 3400 public domain titles. The agreement is a hybrid of NetLibrary's ownership and lease models, with NoWAL owning an agreed percentage of the content at the end of the agreement and able to refresh a proportion of the content each year. The 12,000 titles were selected by participating libraries and are available to up to three simultaneous users per title from any member library. Costs were shared among the participating members pro rata according to the number of full-time equivalent (FTE) students.

This arrangement is significantly different from the general run of consortium activity, approaching the North American model. It embodies a high degree of collaboration through deep resource sharing, with institutions committing to a three-year agreement and sacrificing some institutional autonomy. The potential benefits, in terms of the availability to all students and staff of the participating institutions of over 15,000 titles, are significant, provided that the content is appropriate. It will be very interesting to chart the progress of the agreement as reflected in the usage of the titles available.

Service provision

Access schemes have been part of collaborative provision for many years and are particularly important for distance learners. One of the longest established at the national level is the SCONUL Higher Education Vacation Access Scheme. All SCONUL member libraries, covering the whole of the UK and Ireland as well, participate. Undergraduates and postgraduates on taught courses are eligible for reference-only access to the libraries of other SCONUL members during vacations. This scheme seems relatively restricted in the light of recent developments, but reflects the fears long prevalent that, particularly in metropolitan areas with large and diverse student populations, some libraries could be swamped by demand from external students when provision for their own students is already stretched.

Two other schemes have been introduced in recent years. UK Libraries Plus has 138 participating HEIs. It is open to staff and to students on HE award-bearing courses of one year's duration or more. It provides access for all staff and students, borrowing rights for part-time and distance students and for students on placements of six weeks' duration or more. Although building gradually, this scheme has demonstrated that the fears of 'swamping' just outlined are not warranted in practice, and has attracted more and more libraries as members. SCONUL Research Extra has 139 SCONUL members participating. It provides access and borrowing rights for both academic staff and research (but not taught) postgraduates. Taken together these schemes provide wide reciprocal access and borrowing rights to the majority of students and staff of the majority of HEIs in the UK.

These national schemes are in some measure an extension and recognition of much long established local and regional practice. The UK Libraries Plus website lists 42 access schemes in the UK. Some, such as Anglia Polytechnic University's, reflect partnerships with FECs; others comprise HEIs and may be local (e.g. AULIC – Avon University Libraries in Co-operation) or regional (e.g. Access West Midlands). Some are based on metropolitan areas and have diverse institutions in membership: Portsmouth Access to Libraries (PAL) includes HE, FEC, public, NHS, special libraries and museums. All offer access to collections; many offer borrowing rights, although these may be restricted to certain classes of user or be by subscription. Most reflect librarians' passion for alphabet soup: BLAG, DIG, LASH, SAIL and TWIRL are worthy of mention.

Reciprocal access schemes are testament to libraries' commitment to a variety of local and regional collaboration, growing from the needs of their users. They tend to be at the co-operation end of the collaboration spectrum, but have provided a climate in which the national schemes could flourish.

Training and other staff activities

Co-operative training is one of the longest established areas of collaboration. MacDougall and Prytherch (1989), for example, offer contributions from 13 training co-operatives active in 1989 – five academic, four public and four geographic. Obvious benefits are access to cheap, relatively local and appropriate courses that an individual library would not be able to mount cost effectively, and the ability to influence the type, level and style of courses provided. Otherwise, libraries have to rely on in-house provision, which in smaller institutions may be minimal, or the (generally expensive) offerings of professional bodies and commercial providers. One intangible benefit, common to many areas of collaboration, is the opportunity to meet colleagues doing similar jobs and to build networks.

One good example of collaboration is the Scottish Academic Libraries Co-operative Training Group (SALCTG) (Ball, 1989). This was set up in 1985 and was open to all the HEIs in Scotland and the NLS, at that time a possible membership of 30. An initial survey of potential members elicited responses from 18 HEIs; these had a total staff base of 760, ranging from the smallest with three staff to the largest with 164. This potential membership offered a large audience and a large pool of expertise.

Some doubts were raised about the commonalities possible between such diverse libraries. However, it was quickly apparent that staff from the smaller institutions, who need to be multi-skilled, could benefit from the same courses as those new to or changing roles in the larger libraries. There was also a common curriculum in areas such as management. Further doubts were expressed about the size of the area to be covered, a spread of about 160 miles. However, many of the institutions are located in the central belt, which has good rail and road links to the north east; one-day courses run in Glasgow or Edinburgh were therefore easily accessible to all members. As SALCTG developed, sub-groupings were established as well, focusing for instance on north-east Scotland.

SALCTG has provided training for all levels of staff. Some courses have been provided by professional trainers, others by the staff of member libraries. All are run on a cost-recovery basis; any surplus generated is kept to a minimum, being returned to the members by underwriting courses. A successful programme of courses is still provided, 20 years after the Group's formation.

A more formal approach is adopted by NoWAL (Harris, 2004), which offers a general training programme, a Certificate in Library and Information Practice

(CLIP), and management themes. The general programme offers about 40 events each year, open to both staff in member libraries and external personnel. The CLIP, which is validated by Greater Manchester Open College Network, is a formal programme split into units of 30 hours' study, assessed by written work, tutor feedback and work-based observation. Credits are awarded at AS-Level standard. Since 2000, there have been 144 registered students gaining 385 credits; 19 have gained the full certificate.

Training co-operatives are obviously well established, but tend to work at the level of collaboration. Examples of sharing a staff resource are much rarer. One occurs in north Wales, where the University of Wales Aberystwyth, the University of Wales Lampeter and Trinity College Carmarthen have jointly appointed a member of staff with responsibility for legal compliance issues such as freedom of information and data protection. This approach seems ideally suited to very specialist activities, making a high level of expertise available cost effectively, provided that institutions can free the appropriate budget and that organizational constraints offer no impediment. It is an alternative to some of the outsourcing arrangements discussed in Chapter 5.

Technical areas

As mentioned in Chapter 4, there are some instances of collaborative purchase of LMSs or indeed of a shared system. However, this practice is more prevalent in public libraries, particularly as a result of the reorganization of local government, which had the effect of splitting smaller unitary authorities from large counties. (The Foursite Consortium of Bath & NE Somerset, North Somerset, Somerset and South Gloucestershire is a good example.)

One live example illustrating in some depth the problems and benefits of technical collaboration in the area of e-learning is again taken from Wales – the HELP Project's e-learning feasibility study (Atkinson, 2004). The study had the objective of taking a content-driven approach to developing a shared portal to digital resources in the environmental sciences; the HEIs collaborating were the University of Glamorgan and the University of Wales Institute Cardiff.

While the feasibility study highlights some technical issues, such as differing approaches to passwords and authentication between the institutions, and the suitability and scalability of the architecture adopted, the non-technical issues that emerge are perhaps more interesting. These include:

- the overwhelming dominance of printed textbooks, with journals, databases and other web-based resources seen by academics as supporting or non-core material
- the availability of some recommended texts at the partner institution, but, surprisingly, not at the recommending institution
- the readiness of suppliers of online resources to offer discounts for joint purchase
- the benefits of collaboration to share subject expertise and the production of supporting materials
- major differences in content between superficially similar courses at the different institutions
- competition between universities where academic content is concerned
- the relationship of the portal to other resource discovery tools, such as OPACs, VLEs, library websites and JISC initiatives, e.g. the Resource Discovery Network.

There are some fundamental problems here, for instance competition between similar institutions and the (over-)reliance of academics on printed textbooks. One lesson is that the process of collaboration can bring unforeseen benefits, not least the highlighting of some crucial questions about the way HEIs and their libraries work.

Project working

A project may be defined as 'a specific activity that involves innovation and change ... and ... has a clear aim, set of outcomes and start and end date (Allan, 2004, 5). Clearly many instances of collaboration, such as CASS and the feasibility study just discussed, fulfil this definition; but perhaps the best known collaborative library projects occurred under the Electronic Libraries Programme (eLib).

eLib

The eLib Programme was established in response to the report of the Joint Funding Councils' Libraries Review Group (1993), chaired by Professor Sir Brian Follett. The Report, universally known as the Follett Report, was influential in unlocking large-scale funding for a capital programme for library buildings and pointing the need for engagement with and development of electronic information resources and provision.

Phases 1 and 2 of eLib ran from 1994 to 1997, with a budget of £15 million funding almost 60 projects in the areas of access to networked resources, on-demand publishing, electronic short-loan collections, electronic document delivery, electronic journals, digitization and images (details are available on the eLib website). An evaluation by ESYS (2000) found that eLib was successful in achieving most of its aims, for instance in engaging the broad HE community. In particular, it provided:

- coherence in developing the field
- comprehensiveness in testing a wide range of models and approaches
- coverage in involving a wide range of HEIs
- analysis of its successes and failures
- practical experience of electronic resources and techniques, and of project working and collaboration.

Phase 3 was another three-year programme, with a budget of over £4 million, which sought to consolidate and extend the benefits of the work of Phases 1 and 2. The areas funded were hybrid libraries, large-scale resource discovery (commonly known as clumps), digital preservation and project continuations from the earlier phases. The evaluation by ESYS (2001) provides some interesting insights, generally endorsed by Pinfield (2001), into the value and potential pitfalls of project and collaborative working:

1 It proved very difficult to produce operational systems or viable products within the life-cycle of the funding. There is a step-change between a working prototype, developed and tested by a few partners, and a fully operational system that can be scaled up and rolled out for use by, say, 150 HEIs. Even where systems or products are to be made available free of charge, they still need significant marketing to ensure take-up by the HE sector.

2 The involvement of commercial partners, while often desirable for the benefits to the project and sector, can be problematic. As is clear from earlier chapters, commercial partners have very different cultures and imperatives from HEIs. It can be important to have clear contractual agreements at the start of a project on the commitments of all parties concerned, including the funder. Ideally there should also be a clear understanding of the ownership of any intellectual property rights and of the realization and apportionment of commercial benefits. Funders may prefer to generate some element of competition by involving more than one supplier; however, many

suppliers may be reluctant to invest under such conditions.

3   Some of the most successful projects were built by pre-existing consortia. Where institutions are already in collaborative and established relationships, there seems to be a greater likelihood of sustainability when the project funding ceases. Such consortia will probably have bid for funding for work that they had already identified as necessary or desirable; there is therefore probably a natural market for take-up and for continuing ownership and championing of the outcomes.

4   The outcomes of individual projects and whole programmes may be very different from those intended. One objective outlined in the Follett Report was cost savings. While ESYS discovered little evidence of such savings as a result of the projects, other outcomes, in terms of functionality and the impetus given to the culture of the electronic library, justify the investment.

Other lessons drawn by Pinfield (2001) are that some projects working across sectors, involving public libraries, have been problematic because of differences of culture, funding and technology; that recruiting and retaining project staff on fixed-term contracts can be difficult; and that often insufficient allowance was made for overhead costs such as secretarial support, accommodation, etc., an indication of lack of experience by libraries in project management.

The final word on eLib should go to Rusbridge (2001), who was Programme Director. He endorses the view that a finite funded life of three years is too short to take an idea from prototype through implementation to sustainability, and notes the problems of scalability encountered through no fault of their own by projects relying on Z39.50. He too notes that outcomes are not necessarily those planned, citing a project called InfoBike, which 'may have failed in its original terms' but which mutated through various stages into Ingenta, 'now a £100 million quoted company'. He argues that eLib contributed to a major cultural shift in academic libraries and, together with other initiatives such as NESLI, 'can claim a considerable part of the credit for the rapid scholarly move towards wide-spread use of electronic journals'.

Project management

Clearly, given the number and scale of projects, their management is becoming increasingly important as a technique. One can identify the following stages in the project life-cycle:

- project initiation
- planning the project process
- implementing the project
- evaluating and reviewing the project
- disseminating information about the project and its outcomes.

Allan (2004) offers an extensive discussion of all these stages, with numerous live examples, which are not duplicated here. However, there are some particularly important elements of project management that are worthy of highlighting.

Bidding

While the techniques of project management can usefully be applied no matter how large or small the project, they are perhaps most important in projects involving external funding and partners, where the library and its parent institution are accountable to both the funder and the partnership and obliged to disseminate the results of the project to the wider community. The eLib programme is only one example of the bidding culture prevalent in HE and indeed in the public sector as a whole. Brewer (2002) identifies 38 different funding streams for libraries and learning alone, including the JISC, the various lottery funds and the European Union.

Bidding is a time-consuming process, and, if unsuccessful, a disheartening one. One estimate of a typical success rate for bids for research funding is 25%; clearly one needs to maximize one's chances. One pointer to success has been noted in the discussion of the eLib programme: projects stand a greater chance of success if they arise from established partnerships and already identified needs. It can be quite obvious to funders if a consortium has been created simply as a means of gaining funding; such consortia are more likely to experience tensions and problems than those with a track record of working together.

Obviously bids must fit the criteria and requirements of the funder to stand a reasonable chance. Close reading of the funder's documentation is of paramount importance. Many funders will also give feedback to initial enquiries and sometimes on drafts. Bids must also fit the aims and objectives of the library and the HEI in order to gain the necessary internal support.

Enough detail must be provided to convince the funder that the bid is realistic and will deliver what is promised and required. It is useful, even at this preliminary stage, to identify the work packages into which the project will be split: these are the basic building blocks of any project. The work packages should show precisely what tasks are to be undertaken; who will be responsible for managing and performing them; what the costs (staffing and other) are; how long they will take; what the deliverables will be. Obviously the work packages can be altered in the light of the amount of funding received and further research. If worked through sufficiently they will give the applicant a complete picture of the work and costs entailed; they will also give the funder both enough detail to assess the outcomes and a favourable impression of the professionalism of the applicants.

Once funding has been achieved, a well constructed application then forms the basis for defining and planning the project.

General management issues

Of fundamental importance is the management structure, particularly of large projects. This should operate at three levels:

- The top level is the steering group, which provides strategic guidance and comprises a range of internal and external stakeholders. If well chosen, the steering group should also be able to influence the future embedding of the project and its deliverables. It can be particularly important in projects with external funding.
- The second level is the project management group, comprising those involved in the project at a senior level.
- Finally, there is the project team, comprising those who actually make the project happen.

All projects are threatened by risks. These may be technical, for instance if hardware or infrastructure fails; financial, for instance if matching funding is not obtained; process, for instance if key workers leave; or external, for instance if partners are forced to withdraw. Risk management involves identifying risks and estimating their likelihood and impact on the project. Risks that have both high likelihood and high impact need to be eliminated or the project will fail; risks that have a combination of medium and high likelihood and impact need to be carefully managed; risks that have low likelihood and impact need to be monitored.

Projects may also face a range of legal issues. Digitization may raise problems of copyright ownership. Projects that result in products, or significant intellectual property such as software, will have to determine at the outset who owns the rights and in what proportions. Staff employed for a year or more, even on fixed-term contracts, have significant employment rights. In partnerships it is vital to have a formal agreement between all parties setting out rights and obligations in case of disputes and unforeseen problems.

Project planning

The key to successful project planning lies in the work packages; these should be worked out in detail at the project planning stage. They should identify which of the partners has responsibility for the work package, what the tasks are, what the staff and other costs are, the elapsed time needed and what the deliverables are. One essential work package for projects of any size is project management, which obviously runs throughout the project and is the locus for some of the easily forgotten overhead costs of liaison with the funder and partners, running meetings, maintaining accounts and any general admin-istration for the project.

The sample work package in Figure 8.1 (page 139) is taken from the NOF-funded Dorset Coast Digital Archive project. It shows clearly what is to be done, who is responsible, what the deliverables and timescale are, and how quality is to be assured.

The work packages provide the raw material for developing the project schedule, which outlines who does what when. The deliverables in the work packages also point to the project milestones, which are the markers along the path to successful completion of the project.

Partnerships

Clearly partnership working is essential in many projects of any size. It brings great benefits, but potential risks too. These risks may be minimized by:

- setting clear goals and objectives that are owned and shared by all partners
- all partners committing themselves to the project
- all partners sharing the workload, benefiting from the external funding, and making appropriate contributions
- transparent and realistic planning
- clear and open communication between the partners
- a clear framework of management, accountability and responsibility.

Evaluation and dissemination

Evaluation is important not only for the satisfaction of those leading and working on the project, but also for the funder and supporting institution. It will seek to answer questions such as:

- Were the deliverables achieved?
- Were there any unexpected outcomes?
- Was the project completed on time and within budget?
- What was the impact of the project?

Clearly different methods are required to answer these questions.

Each project will provide its own documentation in the form of plans and schedules, minutes of meetings, reports of activity, and spreadsheets of expenditure; the content and form are often prescribed by the funder. Depending on the nature of the project, there may also be a statistical record: number of objects digitized, hits on the website, etc.

Some projects will have tangible deliverables, such as a piece of software or a new building. Other less technical projects will enter the difficult area of measuring impact. This may be done by standard social science techniques such as questionnaires, interviews and focus groups. These techniques require some skill to apply and analyse successfully; they are also time-consuming.

Dissemination is important for the funder, for the institutions involved and personally for those working on the project. It can bring a lot of welcome publicity, enhance reputations and lay the groundwork for obtaining future finding. Obvious means of dissemination are publishing reports and placing articles and conference papers. Some projects, groups of projects or funders also arrange conferences based on project or programme themes.

Sustainability

As noted in the discussion of the eLib programme above, it can be very difficult to transform a funded project into a sustainable service or product. Some lessons can be learned from another major programme involving libraries, NOF-digitise, which provided £50 million to fund a wide range of publicly available content, with the emphasis on digitizing lifelong learning materials – creating digital resources from existing analogue originals and copies. 150 projects were funded across a wide range of predominantly public sector organizations, mainly related

Level	Partner level
Duration	Year 1 months 1, 2 & 3; quarterly thereafter
Objectives	• To consult widely with target user groups to ensure the archive contains unique, relevant and valuable material that meets the needs of its users
	• To monitor and evaluate feedback from site visitors on a quarterly basis
	• To monitor and evaluate marketing activity and marketing effectiveness
	• To develop and track user group profiles
WP manager	J Bloggs
Partners involved	All partners
Tasks	Task 1 Undertake qualitative research study amongst target user groups and partners on the design and development of the the website
	Task 2 Consult widely with partners, user groups and educationalists on the development and presentation of the themes
	Task 3 Consult widely with partners and user groups on the materials to be digitized to ensure there is no overlap
	Task 4 Devise website feedback form/s
	Task 5 Communicate research findings to project partners and user groups
Deliverables	D1 Feedback from user groups and partners on the website design and development
	D2 Feedback from partners, educationalists and schools on the development of the themes
	D3 Quarterly summary of user profiles and comments from feedback forms
Quality assurance methods	• Benchmarking against the Consortium partners
	• Benchmarking against the NOF-digitise projects
Resources	Management time; research staff time; design and printing:
	Total budget: £8000 (NOF contribution £4500)

Figure 8.1 Sample work package of the Dorset Coast Digital Archive Project: Work Package 2, Audience Research

to cultural content. Anderson (2004), Programme Director for the Big Lottery Fund (formerly the New Opportunities Fund (NOF)) identifies the following ways in which the NOF-digitise projects hope to achieve sustainability:

- become a core organizational mechanism, for instance by providing content that supports the core needs of the organization or making a site so well used that the organization and stakeholders value the access to customers that it provides
- generate income through charges, for instance for value-added services or the sale of licences for a unique product
- acquire sponsorship or advertising, for instance where the profile of visitors to the site enables niche marketing of commercial goods and services
- provide services to third-parties, for instance digitizing services
- become a platform for further development, for instance through obtaining further funding from different funders.

Conclusions

Co-operation and collaboration are endemic to libraries. Partnership working at a quite formal level is becoming more widespread, partly as a result of agreements at the institutional level, partly through the bidding culture prevalent in HE and the public sector generally. However, resource sharing, involving a degree of surrendered autonomy, is much less common. It may well increase, as the strong steer from the funding councils towards increasing institutional collaboration takes effect, and as stronger regional alliances are formed.

Regionalization is a factor within the HE sector, within the cultural sector comprising museums, libraries and archives, and at government level through the Regional Assemblies and the powerful Regional Development Agencies. University libraries, with their history of collaboration, are well placed to embrace and profit from regionalization. A more formal regional approach should enable them to work more effectively and efficiently, and to support institutional and national commitments to widening participation through work-based and distance learning. Many initiatives take the form of projects. Sound techniques of project management are an essential skill for library managers.

9
Conclusion

Universities and their libraries exist in a changing and increasingly complex environment. The accent is on celebrating, acknowledging and funding the different missions of universities, on widening participation to all those with the potential to benefit, and on new modes of study and delivery of courses. There will be greater explicit differentiation between institutions, greater freedom and greater collaboration. All institutions are to be rewarded for their different missions; some will be steered towards research while others are steered towards areas such as knowledge transfer. There is to be more emphasis on the regional dimension, both in the provision of HE and in relations with business and the wider community.

As participation increases towards 50% of those aged 18 to 30, it is expected that the bulk of expansion will be through two-year foundation degrees, and that these will be delivered chiefly in FE colleges. They represent a major offering to business, and also to the big public-sector employers, particularly the NHS. FECs also play a major role in widening participation, by supporting under-represented groups, for instance through local opportunities to those studying part-time. Flexibility of learning opportunities, particularly for those in work, is also stressed.

Libraries face change and complexity in the professional dimension too: the information environment is correspondingly fluid. The electronic revolution has introduced much more fluidity into the information chain. Libraries are dealing directly with publishers rather than exclusively with aggregators. There is also the potential for aggregators of content to deal with the end-user rather than with libraries, especially for e-books.

While the Open Access Initiative and institutional repositories may seem a threat to commercial publishers, allowing academics and institutions to circumvent them in the supply chain, there seems little likelihood of the threat becoming a reality. Publishers offer not only dissemination, where institutional repositories can compete, but also validation. Here there are strong institutional and personal pressures and incentives that make validation in established peer-reviewed commercial journals a very desirable commodity.

University libraries today are very much contracting entities. Fewer and fewer functions, such as binding, processing, cataloguing and classification, are carried out in-house; relationships with suppliers are increasingly governed by contracts. In some areas, such as supplier selection or classification, librarians may feel that they are surrendering too much control over professional practice and standards. There is also a perceived danger of becoming too reliant on external agencies: suppliers do go bankrupt; ownership may change. On the other hand, there is obvious advantage in being able to divert staff time from repetitive processes to service that is focused on the user and the particular demands of the library's clientele. All librarians should question the opportunity cost of continuing to select, catalogue and process books and serials in-house, when suppliers will do it more efficiently.

The electronic revolution has also intensified the shift away from buying a product (a hard-copy book or journal) towards buying a service (access to an electronic resource). While the greater accessibility of electronic resources is welcome to librarians and their users, particularly distance learners, whether in work-based learning or in FECs remote from the university campus, there are also restrictions. Access is governed by the terms of licences negotiated with the providers, which may limit the types, purpose and location of use and restrict the classes of user.

The publishers have also been allowed to dictate not only the licence terms but also the business models under which libraries buy access to journal content. The big deal is probably the best known model. While making available large quantities of material, it also forces a library to either buy or cancel the entire content of the monopolist publisher: the monopoly is thereby intensified. It is intensified even further in the case of national deals covering an entire library sector such as HE; this intensification cannot be in the interests of the purchaser. The business models for buying access to e-books are even more fluid, since the market is even less mature. It is perhaps here that libraries have the opportunity to take control and develop models that favour the purchaser rather than the seller.

The widespread subscription to electronic resources has also introduced increasing complexity in terms of systems. The large library management systems were developed to handle high volumes of hard-copy acquisition and lending. They were not designed for the interoperability increasingly demanded in the electronic environment; this interoperability will become more crucial as virtual learning environments become the dominant platform for interaction of learners with teachers and resources.

In this environment it is particularly important for libraries to exert control over their relationships with suppliers and to influence the market place and business models to their advantage. Following the traditional, standard procurement cycle – identifying the need, preparing the specification, finding the supplier, awarding the contract, measuring and monitoring performance – when procuring resources, whether hard-copy or electronic, whether on a regional or national scale, is fundamental to establishing and maintaining this control. The well established regional procurement consortia, singly and in collaboration, with their blend of different types of expertise, are the principal means of doing so.

The commercial relationships outlined above, whether affecting the procurement of resources or of services that are wholly or partially outsourced, are best governed by tight and full specifications of what is to be provided, written into formal agreements. This sort of discipline is also necessary in the relationships increasingly entered by university libraries with partners in collaborative and project working, and with partners in academic provision, such as FECs and the NHS.

HE's relationships with these two sectors are opposite in one fundamental sense. In the so-called franchising arrangement with an FEC, the HEI is the commissioner, while the FEC provides the service required. The relationship is reversed in the other case, with the NHS commissioning a service from the HEI.

There are, however, many similarities. The relationships are governed by agreements entered into at institutional level, which are vital to the university's mission and to its continuing financial health, and which fulfil some of the central requirements of the government's agenda for HE. They require the effective management of partnerships not necessarily sought by the libraries involved. They have to deliver a service meeting high quality standards, generally at a distance from the campus and to students not fitting the traditional pattern of 18–20-year-old entrants to HE.

Common strands in meeting these various requirements are:

- establishing effective partnerships through good communication, through training of staff to overcome differences in culture, perception and practice, and through peripatetic support

- management of the partnership at a strategic level, involving other stakeholders such as academics and academic managers, with representation of library staff in appropriate deliberative and planning committees, but preferably, given the diversity of relationships and institutions, with one senior member of staff having a co-ordinating role
- staff from all libraries involved working together to ensure as far as possible that infrastructure and funding in the non-HE libraries are adequate for supporting the needs of students
- licence constraints restricting access to electronic resources, which are otherwise ideally suited to this type of distributed and distance learning
- collaboration to present to quality assurance agencies a unified view of the service provided.

Regional collaboration and identity are becoming increasingly important for libraries, as HEIs themselves are encouraged to take a regional view of provision and partnership, and as government and official bodies take an explicitly regional focus. Such collaboration by libraries has long been evident, for instance in access schemes to support the distance learner, in training co-operatives and in procurement. The future will see an increase in so-called deep resource sharing, providing greater efficiency and effectiveness at the cost of some loss of autonomy by the individual library.

This rapidly changing environment offers significant opportunities for university libraries to make a major contribution to the development of their institutions and of HE provision, and to shape in their favour the commercial environment in which they operate. This book is offered as a contribution to equipping university librarians with the knowledge, strategies and techniques that will help them to grasp these opportunities.

Appendix

Bournemouth University Library

Checklist to support evaluation of the library services provided by Bournemouth University Partner Colleges

Institution:
Date of Evaluation:

This checklist is available to print out and use on the Facet Publishing website at www.facetpublishing.co.uk/ball/.

Table of Contents

Note: *page numbers relating to the original document are followed by numbers in square brackets relating to this book.*

Acknowledgements

Bournemouth University Library has adapted and developed the LINC Health Panel Accreditation Working Group document for use in evaluating the library services provided by the University's Partner Colleges. We acknowledge the work of that Group in informing this evaluation checklist. We have also drawn on the SCONUL's *Aide-mémoire for assessors when evaluating library and computing services* (SCONUL, 2003) and the Library Association's *Library and learning resources provision for franchised and other collaborative courses* (1999).

Use of the checklist

The Checklist will be given to the Librarians at Partner Colleges for their initial self-assessment. Staff from Bournemouth University Library will then discuss the document during a visit lasting approximately one hour.

The Checklist is divided into three areas:

- Library Strategy, Planning and Liaison
- Resources
- Learning Materials

For each question, there is a statement that reflects an expectation about the service. This is followed by information about suggested evidence that might be used to assess how well the library is achieving the activity described in the statement. NB the list is indicative and all examples are not required to be available.

There are boxes for an Assessee (usually the Library Manager) and an Assessor (from Bournemouth University Library) to write comments. There is also space for recording agreed actions as a result of discussion of how well the library is judged to satisfy the requirements reflected by an individual statement. This will include examples of excellence and good practice.

The results of this evaluation will form the background to any further specific comments, conditions or recommendations that Bournemouth University might agree with the Partner Colleges.

Section 1
Library Strategy, Planning and Liaison

Introduction

Ensuring that library services effectively anticipate and fulfil existing and future information needs requires a clear vision for the service and careful planning to achieve this vision.

The mission and future for the library service should be clearly defined through a business or strategic plan, which reflects the aims of the parent organisation. Quality assurance measures, including performance indicators and user feedback, should be in place for core services. The library should have appropriate communication links within the College and with learning resources staff at Bournemouth University. There should be library service contribution to course planning to ensure the inclusion of information skills training and to ensure that library services support courses of study. The service should be compliant with all relevant legislation.

The standards covered in this section include:

Strategy
Quality, evaluation and feedback
Liaison
Legislation.

Subsection 1.1 Strategy

Statement 1.1.1

The library has written mission statement/aims/objectives reflecting those of the parent organisation and Bournemouth University, which are reviewed regularly by library and senior management.

Evidence

Publications, e.g. annual report, long-term strategic plan, mission statement, annual development/action plan, readers' charter, annually reviewed strategic/business plan. Evidence of user involvement in the process. Evidence of the impact of higher education on service development.

Assessee Comments

Assessor Comments

Agreed Actions

Statement 1.1.2

The library has an appropriate and defined position within the structure of the wider organisation.

Evidence

Reference to service accountability and organisational structure.

Assessee Comments

Assessor Comments

Agreed Actions

Subsection 1.2 Quality, evaluation and feedback

Statement 1.2.1
The library has a current quality assurance programme, which articulates the services to Bournemouth University students.

Evidence
Published policy. Service level agreements. Evidence of regular review. Quality charter. Contribution to external quality assessment procedures. Strategy for communicating to Bournemouth University changes to library services that many affect Bournemouth University students.

Assessee Comments	Assessor Comments

Agreed Actions

Statement 1.2.2
The library maintains activity statistics and performance indicators, which inform the planning, management and development of services and collections.

Evidence
Records. Use made of statistics. Examples of returns, e.g. SCONUL returns. Regular consultation with Bournemouth University students including records of any actions taken, a formal feedback/suggestions scheme.

Assessee Comments	Assessor Comments

Agreed Actions

Subsection 1.3 Liaison

Statement 1.3.1

There is input from the library to course planning, development and delivery, including attendance at validation events where appropriate.

Evidence

Membership of committees or groups. Staff sampling. Information handling skills recognition in curriculum documents. Course programmes. Documentary evidence. Correspondence. Contact with link tutors.

Assessee Comments

Assessor Comments

Agreed Actions

Statement 1.3.2

The library maintains continuing communication with library subject specialists, IT and other learning resources staff at Bournemouth University.

Evidence

Membership of committees or groups. Staff sampling. Documentary evidence. Correspondence.

Assessee Comments

Assessor Comments

Agreed Actions

Subsection 1.4 Legislation

Statement 1.4.1

The library complies with and the staff are aware of legislation and employer policies relating to: copyright, data protection and confidentiality, health and safety, equal opportunities, DDA, SENDA and other relevant legislation.

Evidence

Published policies. Staff sampling. Compliance with internal/external standards. Copies of legislation available. Policy for compliance with DDA and SENDA. COSHH risk assessments. Accident book. Compliance with DSE regulations.

Assessee Comments

Assessor Comments

Agreed Actions

Section 2
Resources

Introduction

To provide an effective and high-quality information service, the library must have adequate financial, staff and technological resources and appropriate accommodation. There should also be a budget for Bournemouth University courses for which the partner institution (preferably through the librarian) is accountable. A staff development programme and appraisal system for library staff should support service delivery. The library should have adequate space, facilities and equipment to create an environment that is comfortable, user-friendly and safe for readers and staff.

The standards covered in this section include:

Finance
Staffing
Accommodation and equipment.

Subsection 2.1 Finance

Statement 2.1.1

The library budget for Bournemouth University courses is separately identifiable and is reported on regularly.

Evidence

Institutional financial management profile. Staff sampling. Budget statements. Annual/monthly financial reports, indicating all appropriate expenditure headings for HE students. Library mechanism for reconciliation of discrepancies.

Assessee Comments

Assessor Comments

Agreed Actions

Statement 2.1.2

The library budget is reviewed annually, taking into account changes such as: income generation, resource costs and inflation, user numbers, courses, academic level, institutional developments and contracts/service level agreements.

Evidence

Written policy. Formula funding. Presentations/bids. Business plan. Costed resource lists relevant to Bournemouth University courses.

Assessee Comments

Assessor Comments

Agreed Actions

Subsection 2.2 Staffing

Statement 2.2.1

The library service is managed and provided by sufficient numbers of appropriately qualified staff.

Evidence

CVs. Membership of appropriate professional bodies. Proof that current professional issues are addressed. Arrangements to assure appropriate cover if staff are absent.

Assessee Comments

Assessor Comments

Agreed Actions

Statement 2.2.2

The library has a staff development programme available to all staff, and time is allocated for staff development activities.

Evidence

Published policy. Designated budget. A programme of continuing professional development. Staff sampling. Staff meetings. Staff development records, e.g. CILIP CPD programme. Study leave records. Organisational policy. Evidence of participation in Investors in People scheme. Membership of professional organisations. Attendance records.

Assessee Comments

Assessor Comments

Agreed Actions

Subsection 2.2 Staffing (cont.)

Statement 2.2.3

There is a regular appraisal/review system in place for all library staff, which includes the identification of training and development needs. There is an effective and thorough induction programme for library staff, appropriate to each post, which covers the department and the wider organisation.

Evidence

Policy statement. Records. Staff sampling. Personal development plans. Job descriptions. Organisational policy.

Assessee Comments

Assessor Comments

Agreed Actions

Subsection 2.3 Accommodation and equipment

Statement 2.3.1

The availability and locations of the services are well matched to the needs of Bournemouth University students.

Evidence

Distance from teaching accommodation. Parking facilities. Physical evidence. User sampling. Published opening hours.

Assessee Comments

Assessor Comments

Agreed Actions

Statement 2.3.2

There are appropriate numbers of study spaces for Bournemouth University students, including areas for quiet and group study.

Evidence

Library plans. Physical evidence, e.g. quiet study area, carrels, group study rooms. Adherence to recognised standards. Ratio of spaces to potential users.

Assessee Comments

Assessor Comments

Agreed Actions

Subsection 2.3 Accommodation and equipment (cont.)

Statement 2.3.3

Users have access to appropriate equipment, including photocopiers and facilities for computing. Support is available at reasonable hours.

Evidence

Physical evidence. Rotas. Equipment renewal policy. Provision for use of laptops, including access to appropriate networks.

Assessee Comments

Assessor Comments

Agreed Actions

Section 3
Learning Materials

Introduction

The core services provided by the library include access to relevant and up-to-date collections of materials, literature searching, current awareness, enquiry, lending and reservation services, and access to other library collections via an inter-lending service. If possible, library resources should be accessible from other locations within the organisation, as well as the library.

The library service should give training and guidance to provide users with the necessary skills to locate and evaluate information.

The standards covered in this section include:

Availability and relevance of learning resources
User support.

Subsection 3.1 Availability and relevance of learning resources

Statement 3.1.1

The library has an adequate range of materials, in adequate numbers and in an appropriate range of media, covering each relevant discipline or subject area, to meet the needs of Bournemouth University students.

Evidence

Published stock or acquisitions policy. Sampling of information from subject specialists, lecturers, QAA/Ofsted assessments and reading lists/core lists. Physical evidence. Appropriate licences to allow off-air recording and the preparation of study packs as appropriate. Account taken of reservation and issue data. Variable loan periods. Information retrieval tools.

Assessee Comments	Assessor Comments

Agreed Actions

Statement 3.1.2

Policies and procedures are in place to ensure the library's collections, including reference materials, remain well balanced, relevant, in good condition, up to date and adequate for the number of Bournemouth University students.

Evidence

New and additional titles added annually. Published weeding and relegation policy. Use of any relevant current core/standard lists. Annual periodicals review. Sampling of publication dates. Withdrawal records. Binding policy. Physical evidence, including the availability of up-to-date reading list material. Feedback.

Assessee Comments	Assessor Comments

Agreed Actions

Subsection 3.1 Availability and relevance of learning resources (cont.)

Statement 3.1.3

Licences permitting, users are able to gain access to a range of electronic information resources from within and without the institution.

Evidence

College catalogue. Databases provided by the College library. Databases provided by the University Library. Licences.

Assessee Comments	Assessor Comments

Agreed Actions

Statement 3.1.4

The library provides appropriate identification, lending, renewal and reservation services for learning materials.

Evidence

Library management system. OPAC. Website. Published policy. Guide to services. Notices. Loan policies that reflect the study patterns of Bournemouth University students.

Assessee Comments	Assessor Comments

Agreed Actions

Subsection 3.1 Availability and relevance of learning resources (cont.)

Statement 3.1.5

The library provides access to alternative collections through catalogues and document delivery services.

Evidence

Access to catalogues from other libraries and networks. Participation in BLDSC or equivalent scheme. Participation in electronic document delivery schemes. Membership of local library networks. Policy. Passport for Bournemouth University students.

Assessee Comments	Assessor Comments

Agreed Actions

Subsection 3.2 User support

Statement 3.2.1

A comprehensive training and advice programme exists to enable Bournemouth University students to exploit learning resources effectively. The programme covers a wide range of skills relating to information retrieval, data management, critical appraisal and evaluation, and application of research findings.

Evidence

Induction programme. Supplementary programme. Enquiry service. Published evidence. Documentary evidence, e.g. hand-outs, worksheets, help guides.

Assessee Comments

Assessor Comments

Agreed Actions

Statement 3.2.2

A training programme exists for academic staff to heighten awareness of library provision.

Evidence

Documentary evidence, e.g. hand-outs. Published evidence.

Assessee Comments

Assessor Comments

Agreed Actions

Notes

A Checklist to Support Evaluation of the Library Services provided by Bournemouth University Partner Colleges

Checklist Visit Record

Name of Library or Information Service	
Date of Visit	

Names of Library or Information Staff Involved

Name   Signature

Names of Assessors

Name & Position   Signature

Appendix A
List of abbreviations used in the checklist

BLDSC	British Library Document Supply Centre
COSHH	Control of Substances Hazardous to Health
CILIP	Chartered Institute of Library and Information Professionals
CPD	continuing professional development
DDA	Disability Discrimination Act
DSE	display screen equipment
EU	European Union
HE	higher education
ILL	inter-library loan
IT	information technology
JANET	Joint Academic Network
QAA	Quality Assurance Agency
SCONUL	Society of College, National and University Libraries
SENDA	Special Educational Needs and Disability Act 2001

Acronyms and abbreviations

AULIC	Avon University Libraries in Co-operation
BLAG	Bolton Libraries Access Group
CALIM	Consortium of Academic Libraries in Manchester
CASS	Collaborative Academic Store for Scotland
CILIP	Chartered Institute of Library and Information Professionals
CLIP	Certificate in Library and Information Practice
CPD	continuing professional development
CPI	Capital Planning Information Ltd
CSU	California State University
CyMAL	Museums, Archives and Libraries Wales
DCMS	Department for Culture, Media and Sport
DIG	Derbyshire Information Group
DoH	Department of Health
DSW	Dorset, South Somerset and South Wiltshire Higher Education Partnership
EDI	electronic data interchange
eLib	Electronic Libraries Programme
FD	foundation degree
FE	further education
FEC	further education college
FTE	full-time equivalent
HE	higher education
HEFCE	Higher Education Funding Council for England
HEFCW	Higher Education Funding Council for Wales
HEI	higher education institution
HELICON	Health Libraries and Information Confederation
HELP	Higher Education Libraries in Partnership
ICT	information and communications technology
JACC	Journal Access Core Collection
JANET	Joint Academic Network
JISC	Joint Information Systems Committee

LASH	Libraries Access Sunderland Scheme
LINC	Library and Information Co-operation Council
LMS	library management system
MARC	machine-readable cataloguing
MLA	Museums, Libraries and Archives Council
MLE	managed learning environment
MPET	Multi-Professional Education and Training
NeLH	National Electronic Library for Health
NEYAL	North East and Yorkshire Academic Libraries
NHS	National Health Service
NHSU	NHS University
NIACE	National Institute of Adult and Continuing Education
NLH	National Library for Health
NLS	National Library of Scotland
NOF	New Opportunities Fund
NoWAL	North West Academic Libraries
PAL	Portsmouth Access to Libraries
PDA	personal digital assistant
PEAK	Pricing Electronic Access to Knowledge
PFI	Private Finance Initiative
PSLI	Pilot Site Licence Initiative
PSRB	Professional Statutory and Regulatory Body
QAA	Quality Assurance Agency
RSLG	Research Support Libraries Group
RSLP	Research Support Libraries Programme
SAIL	Shropshire Access to Information for Learning
SALCTG	Scottish Academic Libraries Cooperative Training Group
SCONE	Scottish Collections Network
SCONUL	Society of College, National and University Libraries
SED	self-evaluation document
SHEFC	Scottish Higher Education Funding Council
SPARC	Scholarly Publishing and Academic Resources Coalition (generally known by its acronym)
TWIRL	Tyne and Wear Information Resources for Learning
UHSL	University Health Sciences Librarians
UK	United Kingdom
UKCC	United Kingdom Central Council for Nursing, Midwifery and Health Visiting
VAT	value added tax
VLE	virtual learning environment

| WHELF | Welsh Higher Education Libraries Forum |
| WILIP | Wider Libraries Programme |

Bibliography

Publications

Allan, B. (2004) *Project Management: tools and techniques for today's ILS professional*, London, Facet Publishing.

Anderson, C. (2004) Approaches to Sustaining Lottery Funded Digitisation Projects. In *Collaboration for Sustainability: making cultural and heritage projects viable long term*, www.bournemouth.ac.uk/library/collab_sustain.html.

Armstrong, C. and Lonsdale, R. (2003) *The e-Book Mapping Exercise: draft report on Phase 1*, London, JISC, www.jisc.ac.uk/coll_ebookstudy1.html.

Arnold, K. (2002) The Partnership Experience: De Montfort University and its associate libraries network, *SCONUL Newsletter*, **27**, 49–54.

Atkinson, J. (2004) *Higher Education Libraries in Partnership (HELP) Project: part 3: e-learning feasibility study*, unpublished, Wales Higher Education Libraries Forum.

Ball, D. (1987) Conspectus in Scotland, *Westwords*, **2**, 4–5

Ball, D. (1989) The Scottish Academic Libraries Co-operative Training Group. In MacDougall, A. and Prytherch, R. (eds) *Co-operative Training in Libraries*, Aldershot, Gower, 79–91.

Ball, D. (1996) The Big Flame: a model for a universal full-text electronic library of research. In *Libraries and Associations in the Transient World: new technologies and new forms of cooperation: conference proceedings: third international conference 'Crimea 96'*, Moscow, National Public Library of Science and Technology, vol. 2, 112–15.

Ball, D. et al. (2002) *A Study of Outsourcing and Externalisation by Libraries, with Additional Reference to the Museums and Archives Domains*, Resource research project LIC/RE/108, BUOPOLIS, 5, Bournemouth, Bournemouth University.

Beard, J. (1995) An Organisational Passport to Library Services for Nursing Students. In Rowlands, J. (ed.) *Empowering the Library User: passports to information: proceedings of a seminar held in Stamford, Lincolnshire, 26*

April 1995, Stamford, CPI.

Bide, M. (1998) *Business Models for Distribution, Archiving and Use of Electronic Information: towards a value chain perspective*, unpublished, ECUP+.

BioMed Central (2003a) *UK Research, Accessible for Free, for Everyone*, www.biomedcentral.com/info/about/pr-releaese?pr=20030617/.

BioMed Central (2003b) *Australia Opens Access to Research with BioMed Central*, www.biomedcentral.com/info/about/pr-releaese?pr=20031208/.

Black, C. and Bury, R. (2004) All for One, One for All: collaboration between NHS and higher education in establishing provision of a multi-disciplinary, hospital-based library and information services, *Health Information and Libraries Journal*, **21**, (June supplement), 39–45.

Bordeianu, S. and Benaud, C. (1997) Outsourcing in American Libraries: an overview, *Against the Grain*, **9** (5), 1, 16, 18, 20.

Boss, R. W. (1999) Guide to Outsourcing in Libraries, *Library Technology Reports*, **34** (5), whole issue.

Breeding, M. (2004) Integrated Library Software: a guide to multiuser, multifunctional systems, *Library Technology Reports*, **40** (1), whole issue.

Brewer, S. (2002) *Overview of Funding Streams for Libraries and Learning in England*, London, Resource, www.mla.gov.uk/.

Brown, L. A. and Forsyth, J. H. (1999) The Evolving Approval Plan: how academic librarians evaluate services for vendor selection and performance, *Library Collections, Acquisitions and Technical Services*, **23**, 231–77.

Capel, S., Banwell, L. and Walton, G. (1997) Library and Information Services to Support the Education and Development of Nurses: the management of co-operation and change – a clash of two cultures?, *Health Libraries Review*, **14**, 233–45.

Capital Planning Information (1999) *Outsourcing Book Selection: supplier selection in public libraries: a report to the British National Bibliography Research Fund*, Library and Information Commission research report 20, London, Library and Information Commission.

Chapman, A. and Spiller, D. (2000) *Trend Analysis of Monograph Acquisitions in Public and University Libraries in the UK*, LISU occasional paper 25, Loughborough, Library and Information Statistics Unit, Department of Information Science, Loughborough University.

Chartered Institute of Library and Information Professionals (2003) *UK Survey of Library and Learning Resource Provision in Further Education Colleges, 2003*, London, CILIP.

Childs, S. and Banwell, L. (2001) *Partnerships in Health: effective access models to higher education and National Health Service libraries for health professionals and students: a British Library project funded under the Co-operation and Partnership Programme: final report, February 2001,* Newcastle upon Tyne, Information Management Research Institute, School of Information Studies, University of Northumbria.

CIPFA Statistical Information Service (2004) *Public Library Statistics 2002–03: actuals,* London, CIPFA.

Committee on Higher Education (1963) *Higher Education: report of the Committee appointed by the Prime Minister under the Chairmanship of Lord Robbins 1961–1963,* Robbins Report, Cmnd 2154, London, HMSO.

Crawford, J. (2002) A Study of Issues in Administering Library Services to Nursing Studies Students at Glasgow Caledonian University, *Health Information and Libraries Journal,* **19,** 90–7.

Dale, P., Holland, M. and Matthews, M. (eds) (2005) *Rethinking Libraries: subject support in academic libraries,* Aldershot, Ashgate.

Department for Education and Employment (1998) *The Learning Age: higher education for the 21st century: response to the Dearing Report,* London, TSO.

Department for Education and Skills (2003) *The Future of Higher Education,* Cm 5735, London, TSO.

Department of Health (1999) *Making a Difference: strengthening the nursing midwifery and health visiting contribution to health and healthcare,* London, HMSO.

Dubberley, R. A. (1998) Why Outsourcing is Our Friend, *American Libraries,* (January), 72–4.

Edmonds, D. (2003) Portfolio for Success, *Library and Information Update,* **2** (7), 50–1.

Education for Change, University of Stirling Centre for Publishing Studies and University of Stirling Information Services (2003) *A Strategy for the Future for Electronic Textbooks in UK Further and Higher Education: a study prepared for the Joint Information Systems Committee (JISC) E-Books Working Group,* London, JISC.

Eduserv (2003) *Chest Agreements: types of user access,* www.eduserv.org.uk/chest/user-access.html/.

Eduserv (2004) *Chest General Licence Conditions (Datasets),* www.chest.ac.uk/support.html/.

ESYS (2000) *Summative Evaluation of Phases 1 and 2 of the eLib Initiative: final report,* Guildford, ESYS.

ESYS (2001) *Summative Evaluation of Phase 3 of the eLib Initiative: final report,* Guildford, ESYS.

Fisher, S., Delbridge, R. and Lambert, S. (2001) *Harmonising the Process of*

Procuring Library Management Systems: a feasibility study, LIC research report 99, London, Resource.

Foy, M., Spencer, C. and Ball, D. (2002) Access and Identity: delivering HE in the FE environment, *Relay: UC&R*, **54**, 9–11.

Gannon-Leary, P., Wakeham, M. and Walton, G. (2003) Making a Difference to Nurse Education: the impact on HE libraries, *Journal of Librarianship and Information Science*, **35** (1), 31–46.

Gasson, C. (2002) Holding on to Family Values: Christopher Gasson talks to Philip Blackwell about his commitment to the family firm, *The Bookseller*, (8 November), 20–2.

Gibbons, S., Peters, T. A. and Bryan, R. (2003) *E-book Functionality: what libraries and their patrons want and expect from electronic books*, LITA Guide 10, Chicago, LITA.

Gillies, A. (2000) Information Support for General Practice in the New NHS, *Health Information and Libraries Journal*, **17** (2), 91–6.

Goodall, D. (1996) Academic Franchising: some pointers for improving practice, *Library Management*, **17**, 4–9.

Goodall, D. and Brophy, P. (1997) *A Comparable Experience?: library support for franchised courses in higher education*, British Library Research and Innovation Report 33, Preston, Centre for Research in Library and Information Management.

Grimwood-Jones, D. (1994) TUPE or not TUPE?: successful contracting for the public sector, *Managing Information*, **1** (3), 26–7.

Guédon, J.-C. (2001) In Oldenburg's Long Shadow: librarians, research scientists, publishers, and the control of scientific publishing, *ARL Proceedings*, **138** (May), www.arl.org/arl/proceedings/138/guedon.html/.

Hamaker, C (2003) Quantity, Quality and the Role of Consortia. In *What's the Big Deal?: journal purchasing – bulk buying or cherry picking?: strategic issues for librarians, publishers, agents and intermediaries: ASA 2003 conference*, www.subscription-agents.org/conference/200302/chuck.hamaker.pps/.

Harris, C. (2004) NoWAL Developments: staff development and training, procurement of e-products. In *Regional Collaboration and Academic Libraries: a state of the art conference: WHELF, Tuesday 21 September 2004, Cardiff*, unpublished.

Healy, L. W. (1999) New Bottles for Old Wine?: California State University initiates an electronic core journals collection, *Educom Review*, **34** (3), www.educause.niss.ac.uk/ir/library/html/erm9935.html.

HEFCE (2002) *Franchised Students 2000–01: students registered at one institution and taught at another*, 2002/51, Bristol, HEFCE.

HEFCE (2003a) *Supporting Higher Education in Further Education Colleges: a guide for tutors and lecturers*, 2003/15, Bristol, HEFCE.

HEFCE (2003b) *Realising a Vision for Higher Education: HEFCE annual review for 2002–03*, Bristol, HEFCE.

HEFCE (2004a) *HEFCE Strategic Plan for 2003–08 (Revised April 2004)*, 2004/17, Bristol, HEFCE.

HEFCE (2004b) *Practical Guide to PFI for Higher Education Institutions*, rev. edn, 2004/11, Bristol, HEFCE.

HEFCE (2004c) *Collaboratively Taught Students 2001–02: students registered at one institution but taught at another*, 2004/02, Bristol, HEFCE.

Herman, C. and Ward, S. (2004) *The NHS Library Policy Review: developing the strategic roadmap: a report by TFPL Ltd for the NHS*, London, TFPL Ltd.

Hewlett, J. (1992) Who Uses NHS Libraries?: preliminary results from a survey of postgraduate medical libraries in North East Thames, *Health Libraries Review*, **9**, 66–76.

Hewlett, J, and Walton, G. (2001) Assessing the Quality of Library and Information Services for United Kingdom Health Professionals and Students: a comparison of the National Health Service and higher education approaches and the way forward, *Performance Measurement and Metrics*, **2** (1), 81–95.

Higher Education Consultancy Group and CHEMS Consulting (2002) *Report to the RSLP on Barriers to Resource Sharing among Higher Education Libraries*, unpublished, RSLP.

Higher Education in the United Kingdom: guide (2004), Bristol, HEFCE.

Houghton, J. (2000) *Economics of Scholarly Communication: a discussion paper prepared for the Coalition for Innovation in Scholarly Communication*, Canberra, The Coalition, www.caul.edu.au/cisc/EconomicsScholarlyCommunication.pdf/.

House of Commons Science and Technology Committee (2004) *Scientific Publications: free for all?: tenth report of Session 2003–04*, London, TSO.

Howley, S. and Stevens, A. (2003) *WILIP: summary report and next steps*, London, Resource.

Hutton, W. (2000) How Protesters Fuelled a Very 21st-Century Crisis, *Guardian*, (17 September), 16.

Jenkins, P. O. (2003) The Approval Plan: what's in it for small OhioLINK libraries?, *Library Collections, Acquisitions, & Technical Services*, **27** (2), 179–81.

JISC (2000) *Managed Learning Environments (MLEs) in Further Education: progress report*, JISC Circular 7/00, London, JISC.

Joint Funding Councils' Libraries Review Group (1993) *Report,* Follett Report, Bristol, HEFCE.

Kensler, E. (2004) *Higher Education Libraries in Partnership (HELP) Project: part 2: collaboration review*, unpublished, Wales Higher Education Libraries Forum.

Kensler, E. et al. (2004) *Higher Education Libraries in Partnership (HELP) Project: part 4: journals case study*, unpublished, Wales Higher Education Libraries Forum.

Key Perspectives (2004) *JISC/OSI Journal Authors Survey: report*, Truro, Key Perspectives.

KPMG and Capital Planning Information Ltd (1995) *DNH Study: contracting-out in public libraries*, London, KPMG.

Library Association (1999) *Library and Learning Resources Provision for Franchised and other Collaborative Courses*, London, Library Association.

Lund University Library (2004) *Directory of Open Access Journals*, www.doaj.org/.

MacDougall, A. and Prytherch, R. (eds) (1989) *Co-operative Training in Libraries*, Aldershot, Gower.

Marcum, J. W. (1998) Outsourcing in Libraries: tactic, strategy, or 'meta-strategy'?, *Library Administration & Management,* **12** (1), 15–25.

Mark Ware Consulting (2004) *Pathfinder Research on Web-based Repositories: final report*, [London?], Publisher and Library/Learning Solutions.

McCabe, M. J. (2000) *Academic Journal Pricing and Market Power: a portfolio approach*, www.prism.gatech.edu/%7Emm284/JournPub.PDF.

Miers, M. (2002) Nurse Education in Higher Education: understanding cultural barriers to progress, *Nurse Education Today*, **22**, 211–19.

Missingham, R. (n.d.) Outsourcing and Libraries: a threat or promise?, *ASL article*, www.nla.gov.au/flin/outsourc/asl.html.

Muir, L. and Fishwick, F. (2000) *Key Issues in Public Library Book Supply: a study conducted for Book Industry Communication and the National Acquisitions Group*, Library and Information Commission Research Report 46, London, Book Industry Communication.

National Committee of Inquiry into Higher Education (1997) *Higher Education in the Learning Society*, Dearing Report, London, HMSO.

National Institute of Adult and Continuing Education et al. (2003) *Review of Indirect Funding Agreements and Arrangements between Higher Education Institutions and Further Education Colleges*, HEFCE Issues Paper 57, Bristol, HEFCE.

Naylor, C. (2000) When the Supplier Selects, *The Bookseller*, (18 February), 28–9.

NHS Executive (1997) *Library and Information Services*, HSG(97) 47, London, NHS Executive.

NHSU (2003a) *About Us FAQs*, www.nhsu.nhs.uk/web portal/about us/faqs.jsp/.

NHSU (2003b) *Draft Strategic Plan 2003–2008*, London, NHSU, www.nhsu.nhs.uk/webportal/aboutus/index.jsp.

Nicholas, D. and Huntington, P. (2002) Big Deals: results and analysis from a pilot analysis of web log data: report for the Ingenta Institute. In *The Consortium Site Licence: is it a sustainable model?: edited proceedings of a meeting held on 24th September 2002 at the Royal Society, London*, Oxford, Ingenta, 121–59.

Nicholson, C. (2004) CASS: collaborative academic store for Scotland pilot. In *Regional Collaboration and Academic Libraries: a state of the art conference: WHELF, Tuesday 21 September 2004, Cardiff*, unpublished.

O'Looney, J. (1998) *Outsourcing State and Local Government Services: decision-making strategies and management*, Quorom, London.

Pinfield, S. (2001) *Beyond eLib: lessons from Phase 3 of the Electronic Libraries Programme*, www.ukoln.ac.uk/services/elib/papers/other/intro.html.

Porter, S. (2002) Virtual Learning Environments and Managed Learning Environments, *Relay: UC&R*, **53**, 4–6.

Poynder, R. (2002) A True Market Failure: Professor Mark McCabe talks about problems in the STM publishing industry, *Information Today*, **19** (11), www.infotoday.com/it/dec02/poynder.htm.

Quality Assurance Agency (2003) *Handbook for Major Review of Healthcare Programmes*, London, QAA, www.qaa.ac.uk/health/health_home.htm.

Quality Assurance Agency (2004) *Code of Practice for the Assurance of Academic Quality and Standards in Higher Education: section 2: collaborative provision, and flexible and distributed learning (including e-learning): draft for consultation – January 2004*, www.qaa.ac.uk.

Reidelbach, J. H. and Shirk, G. M. (1984) Selecting an Approval Plan Vendor II: comparative vendor data, *Library Acquisitions: Practice and Theory*, **8** (3), 157–202.

Research Support Libraries Group (2003) *Research Support Libraries Group Final Report*, unpublished, RSLG.

Rusbridge, C. (2001) After eLib, *Ariadne*, **26**, www.ariadne.ac.uk/issue26/

Ryland, J. (2004) Supporting Staff and Students: the regional experience. In *Access and Identity 2: challenges of delivering HE learning resources in the FE environment*, www.bournemouth.ac.uk/library/conference_ai2.html.

SCONUL (2003) *Aide-Mémoire for Assessors when Evaluating Library and Computing Services*, London, SCONUL.

SCONUL Advisory Committee on Health Sciences (2003) *Funding of HE Library Services to Support the NHS: a report of a survey 2003*, London, SCONUL.

Scottish Funding Councils for Further and Higher Education (2003) *Aiming Further and Higher: joint corporate plan 2003–06*, Edinburgh, The Councils.

Stanford University (2004) *Faculty Senate Minutes February 19 Meeting*, news-service.stanford.edu/news/2004/february25/minutes-225.html.

Thomson ISI (2004) *The Impact of Open Access Journals: a citation study for Thomson ISI*, unpublished, The Thomson Corporation.

Thornhill, J. (2003) *Users First: removing barriers to knowledge access across HE and the NHS: a report for the NHS/HE Forum*, London, NHS/HE Forum.

United Kingdom Central Council for Nursing, Midwifery and Health Visiting (UKCC) (1986) *Project 2000: a new preparation for practice*, London, UKCC.

United Kingdom Central Council for Nursing, Midwifery and Health Visiting (UKCC) (1999) *Fitness for Practice*, London, UKCC.

Weaver, M. et al. (1999) Centralised Classification of Library Materials: a benchmarking study, *Library and Information Research News*, **23** (74), 23–32.

Wellcome Trust (2004) *Costs and Business Models in Scientific Research Publishing: a report commissioned by the Wellcome Trust*, London, The Trust.

Willett, C. (1998) Consider the Source: a case against outsourcing materials selection in academic libraries, *Collection Building*, **17** (2), 91–5.

Young, J. R. (2004) Google Teams up with 17 Colleges to Test Searches of Scholarly Materials, *Chronicle of Higher Education*, (9 April), chronicle.com/free/2004/04/20040409oln.htm.

Websites

ArXiv
   http://arxiv.org.
California State University, Journal Access Core Collection (JACC)
   www.csuchico.edu/lacq/jacc.htm.
CogPrints
   http://cogprints.ecs.soton.ac.uk/.
Eduserv/CHEST
   www.eduserv.org.uk/chest/.

eLib
    www.ukoln.ac.uk/services/elib/.
Foursite Consortium
    www.foursite.somerset.gov.uk/.
HEFCE
    www.hefce.ac.uk/.
JISC
    www.jisc.ac.uk/.
NeLH (National Electronic Library for Health)
    www.nelh.nhs.uk.
NESLi2
    www.nesli2.ac.uk/.
NHSU
    www.nhsu.nhs.uk/.
OpenRFP
    www.openrfp.com/.
Public Library of Science
    www.publiclibraryofscience.org/.
PubMed Central
    www.pubmedcentral.nih.gov/.
SCONUL
    www.sconul.ac.uk/.
UHSL (University Health Science Librarians Group)
    www.uhsl.ac.uk/.
UK Libraries Plus
    www.uklibrariesplus.ac.uk/.
UMSLG (University Medical School Librarians Group)
    www.umslg.ac.uk/.
University of Michigan PEAK Project
    www.lib.umich.edu/retired/peak/.

Index